I have known Susan Sohn for most c[...] consistently thought out of the box [...] She's kind and passionate, and I have no doubt the words in *True You* will impact a lot of people. Additionally, Susan helped me convince my wife to marry me. It's cool to see her make the shift from matchmaking to author!

—CARL LENTZ, author of *Own the Moment*, pastor of Hillsong Church, New York City

Susan Sohn is someone who asks the deep, personal questions most of us àre too afraid to ask. She has the ability to identify what is really going on when it comes to the things that hold us back from being our true selves or living a brave and flourishing life. Through conversations with hundreds of women from around the globe, Susan shares stories and research that peel back the lies layer by layer to reveal the truth at the core of our fears. In this book, as she does in life, Susan assures readers that they are not alone, and she provides practical steps to obtaining freedom and breakthrough.

—VICKIE REDDY, executive producer, The Justice Conference, USA

For years I had the extreme pleasure of sharing life and proximity with Susan Sohn and her family before their move to a new city and adventure. In working alongside her, I only knew a girl who was passionate about making a positive difference in this world. This book and labor of love is about value, worth, and authenticity and is full of compassion, inspiration, and insightful wisdom. I trust it will not only bless you but also those within your world of influence.

—BOBBIE HOUSTON, global co-senior pastor of Hillsong Church

After countless hours and hundreds of interviews with women all across the world, Susan has woven her own pain, heart, and story into the mix of *True You* to deliver a potent tapestry of light and shade and the powerful truth that we are more—more than enough because we have a God who is.

—SUSANNA BATEMAN, cofounder of Little Miracles
Early Childhood Centres

True You is the call to action every woman needs to hear: Your time is now. You are more than enough. You don't belong on the sidelines. Make a choice to gather with people who celebrate you, not tolerate you. Susan Sohn, through her compelling storytelling, genuinely gives us the courage to face the truth of our lives, to dig deep, and discover a rich inner life. *True You* is one of the most inspiring books I have ever read!

—WENDY SIMPSON OAM, FAICD, Australian Businesswoman's Hall
of Fame, director of World Vision Australia, founding chairman
of Springboard Enterprises Australia, and founder of Telstra
Australian Business Awards

In the pages of *True You*, you will find a soul sister and fast friend in Susan Sohn. Even though she and I live thousands of miles from one another, her heart, words, and life resonate so deeply with mine, and I'm sure they will with yours too. Love, truth, vulnerability, authenticity, beauty, and freedom echo from her life and spill out onto each page. You won't be able to put this book down as you go on a genuine journey of discovery to find out that you are so much more than you've ever believed.

—ANDI ANDREW, author of *She Is Free* and *Fake or Follower*,
cofounder of Liberty Church, New York City

In *True You*, Susan Sohn has gifted us with a truth-telling work that speaks to the heart of a woman's identity and her story. It's raw and honest yet tender and life-affirming. *True You* is for anyone who feels that she has lost sight of her true identity. Susan's words will tell it to you straight and lovingly. And she'll help you rediscover how to live courageously in total freedom.

—Jo Saxton, speaker, *Lead Stories* podcast host, author of *The Dream of You*

For twenty years I have known Susan Sohn as Mum. Although that role is important, there are infinite ways to describe her. To name a few, she is brave, strong, compassionate, wise, and loyal to her core. Not only do these characteristics shine through her life and very being, but they are also seen through her writing. Her book *True You* celebrates truth by speaking honestly about the pain and darkness that can sometimes be the human experience, and it highlights the beauty of strength and resilience— something I have watched her display throughout her life. For this reason, I am honored to be her daughter. Her book encourages others to shine light through darkness and learn to be compassionate, not only to others but also to themselves. From an early age I learned that Mum always has the time to listen, the door is always open, the kettle is on the boil, and there is always a seat at the table. It's that very reason this book was written. The stories. The pain. The beauty. The life. All heard at our kitchen table, whether it be by the phone or in person. She always listens. I hope to be the same. Mum, as you step into your new role as author, stay brave, stay wise, stay compassionate, and keep listening. There are people with stories to tell and people who need to hear them.

—Sophia Sohn, daughter, student, life adventurer

Best friends are those with whom we can be ourselves with raw honesty. In her first book, *True You*, Susan Sohn offers this kind of friendship to all who will come with her on the journey. This is an intimate and authentic account in which Susan speaks from lived experience. We need to hear what she has to say. The pressure to outwardly appear to have the beautiful and perfect life can be as pervasive in the church as it is in the wider culture. When Susan identified and named this truth in her own life, she began a journey toward real freedom—the freedom we are offered in the quiet enjoyment of an honest relationship with Jesus. By sharing what she learned, Susan will help countless people who are living a lie and can't see the way out. Be encouraged! Susan's frank and helpful book points the way to real freedom.

—STEPHEN O'DOHERTY, Christian broadcaster, former New South Wales Member of Parliament

Gritty, honest, and deeply personal, Susan Sohn in *True You* has masterfully woven the narratives of countless women and her own into a common thread—all challenging the lie that we are not enough. *True You* is no-holds-barred and stunningly intimate. It provides a profoundly spiritual approach to the human condition. It's time to start the conversation and get real with one another.

—NICOLE PARTRIDGE, journalist, writer

Wow! What words can describe this book, *True You*? Authentic. Vulnerable. Brilliant. Transformative. Incredibly insightful. Through brave, fierce, and beautifully shared stories, Susan Sohn's book is bound to help women interlock arms and walk each other forward on the path to freedom.

—CARLY THOMSON, writer, speaker, author of the Truth Seekers trilogy, carlythomson.com

In *True You*, Susan Sohn writes from a place of strength and experience. Her very nature and character are defined by resilience, strength, and loyalty. Susan writes with deep understanding, and through her storytelling, she graciously opens a window into the lives of women from around the world. These shared stories speak forth a confidence that we can all make it through whatever we are going through because we are more.

—KATHERINE GAGNE, sister and vice president of
Junior Achievement, Saskatchewan, Canada

Some people walk into your life at exactly the right moment. Susan Sohn was one of these people. Her words have made me cry because they ring true and relevant. Her words make me laugh because they are real and pure joy. She is first and foremost a storyteller, as *True You* shows. And with this collective of women she has bravely bared her soul to, and vice versa, Susan heralds the beginning of a new era—when women are making loud noises without fear and paving their paths, regardless of the turmoil or pain behind them. Thank you, Susan, for your voice. And for your heart.

—CAITLIN ROBSON, media and communications studies graduate

Susan has always been a gatherer of stories and people. Reading this book is like sitting around the campfire with her: intimate, unguarded, and generous. In these pages, you'll find yourself in the stories she shares and the resilience to live your truth like only you can. The contemplative practices Susan teaches will empower you to sort the lies from the truth on your own terms and find life in the middle of where you are right now. Susan is a brave and beautiful friend, and I'm so thankful for her book.

—LIZ MILANI, founder and writer at Pktfuel.com

Susan Sohn is the sort of friend who doesn't bat an eyelid at confessions of stupidity, words spoken in anger, and dumb mistakes. She filmed me and laughed as I fell down a mountain in Bali, but she also attended an appointment with me that was urgently ordered by my doctor to rule out breast cancer. In short, she's the real deal. I have loved walking with her on the road back to self that seems to open up in midlife and sharing tears and moments of clarity with her. I'm so proud of Susan's vulnerable storytelling in *True You*. She is brave and offers her pain to the reader, so that we can find healing. Take a deep breath, know you're not alone, and settle in for some time with a trusted girlfriend.

—JANE CARMODY, longtime friend and fan

I have the pleasure of calling Susan Sohn my friend, a title that she does not take lightly. She is one of those rare people today who, when she steps into your life, actually cares deeply for you. She is one of my dearest friends and has been there with me and our family in the good, the bad, and the ugly. She has encouraged me to take steps in my personal career that I didn't think I was capable of taking. She has cried with me through tough parenting issues and laughed with me over life's mishaps. Her determination to help those around her see their potential and then reach it is simply beautiful, as *True You* shows. I can't wait to see what Susan's next adventure will be as I'm sure she will take it on with grace and guts to achieve it.

—SUZANNE CROCKER, pastor of Hope United,
Santa Monica, California

TRUE YOU

Finding Beauty in Authenticity

SUSAN J. SOHN

BroadStreet
PUBLISHING

BroadStreet Publishing® Group, LLC
Savage, Minnesota, USA
BroadStreetPublishing.com

True You: Finding Beauty in Authenticity

978-1-4245-5451-5 (softcover)
978-1-4245-5452-2 (e-book)

Stock or custom editions of BroadStreet Publishing titles may be purchased in bulk for educational, business, ministry, fundraising, or sales promotional use. For information, please email info@broadstreetpublishing.com.

Cover design by Chris Garborg at garborgdesign.com
Typesetting by Kjell Garborg at garborgdesign.com

Printed in the United States of America
18 19 20 21 22 5 4 3 2 1

To every woman who has ever lifted
another sister up when she's fallen down,
said, "Yes, you can," when they said, "No, I can't,"
and carried them until they could walk.

CONTENTS

FOREWORD

I am really proud of my friend, Susan Sohn. We bonded many years ago when she and Philip had taken the leap from her treasured daily life to attend Bible college on the other side of the world. Susan had the cutest little daughter, Sophia, on her hip, and a contagious love for life and people, which remains with her today. Our friendship has lasted the tests of time, missteps, differences, and distance. Here we are, all these years later, loving and respecting each other's journeys and embracing the things that unite us rather than focusing on the things that have the power to divide.

True You is truly her. As one who has held faithful to her passion to gather others and help them give voice to their pain inside, she has done this with great respect and dignity. She is not writing as one who appeals to you as an expert, but as one who is doing the hard work of digging deep. And no matter what surfaces, she deals with it in the safety of God's profound and abiding love.

The many people she interviewed to see this book come about with a robustness of truth is a true testament to the tenacity in which she has gone after this finished product and a true testament to the willingness she displays to tell real stories from real people—all to bring real help to as many people as she can.

So buckle up! *True You* is not a lighthearted read to tickle your senses, nor is it a piece that condemns any wandering and searching soul. But I think you will feel like you are sitting at Susan's table, surrounded by really good food, having a laugh and maybe a cry, with all of it leading toward embracing your own free and rich soul while giving you tools to ask the real questions that need to be aired along the way.

So here's to you, the reader: May there be greater days ahead—days rich with laughter, food, family, presence, and song, days in which you know who you are and whose you are, the true you. Oh, my friend, the journey is worth it. My greatest prayer is that every person on this journey of life will find their true worth in Christ and, through His love, find their purpose, freedom, and joy.

In the meantime, I would like to say well done, Suzie. I think you are about to embark on the journey of a lifetime.

Love,

Darlene Zschech
Wife and mum, friend and co-laborer,
senior pastor of Hope UC

BEFORE WE BEGIN

Much of the writing of this book has taken place during a truly transformational journey that my husband and I have embarked on. It is based on Christian contemplative spirituality involving meditation and an experienced union with God.

Early on in our spiritual journey, due to what could only be termed as a miraculous change in our ourselves and our marriage, we decided to start a series of gatherings, firstly in our home, and then more in other places. We named this The Gathering Cloud. We meet to commune with God and to be community to one another.

We are made from love and for love. As we move toward God, He moves us toward becoming a kinder and more compassionate people. I would not be exaggerating to say that all my notions of my self-identity have been challenged and gently transformed from my very core being, connected to the ultimate reality: God.

The Gathering Cloud has two expressions now: We host monthly meetings in various homes, where we follow a contemplative liturgy of spiritual practices, sometimes outdoors around a roaring fire, and we host a weekly guided meditation group at our local studio.

At the end of each chapter of this book, there is a practice of Retreating congruent with the content of the chapter theme. Some of the practices are based on those we do at The Gathering Cloud. We hope they are as helpful for you as they are for us.

As part of my work, I run something called GetRealLive—an online, podcast, social media, and event community. We offer multi-day retreats where participants attend an immersive experience of food, fun, and deep inner work. Some of the stories and reflections in this book are from GetRealLive retreats.

INTRODUCTION

When I started this project, I was struggling. I was in my mid-forties, had a thousand things to do, and time was zipping by. Chaos was the ruling theme of my life, and I knew I was not alone.

Having lived in a few different places in the world and being a generally social type who is always up for a deep and meaningful conversation, I started noticing the "chatter" on Facebook and Instagram. I don't mean the polished top-5-percent-of-life highlights, but the messages in the dark of night that showed me many of the women in my world were struggling too.

I started to open up to others and share my truth over coffee, glasses of wine, phone conversations, text messages, and social media. The more real I was, the more real everyone else was. It was like we gave permission to each other to be vulnerable.

Curiosity started to arise in me. What if I asked hundreds of women around the world of all stripes and colors about their life, their stories, and their struggles to see if there were experiences common to all of us. As someone who interviews people on a regular basis, I decided to embark on a one-year journey of speaking with women to find our collective truth in our individual narratives. I put out a post on social media inviting women to schedule a thirty-minute Skype conversation with me, in anonymity, where I would ask them a series of questions and let the conversations flow freely from there.

Hundreds of women responded.

Their stories are what have made it possible for me to write this book. This writing coincided with a deep spiritual journey of inner transformation that has changed so many things about my life, my marriage, and my family. It has changed the place from which I live and the way I love. It has transformed my sense of self and worth, for which I am so grateful. You will read much of my story in these pages.

Woven into the fabric of this book are the stories of brave and courageous women, in addition to my own stories and reflections. There are also some practices that have helped me, which I hope will help you too, as we navigate this life of ours that we share in this time and space.

And as we begin, I would like to say this: You are more. You are more than enough.

A Brief Hello

My husband, Philip, and I were living in Australia when we started having children. Our young family was growing, and I realized that with the birth of each child came more and more questions from my friends. I found this strange considering Philip and I were raising children in a country where we had no family support and surviving on the help of the very friends who continued to ask questions. They would ask me things like, "Why are you disciplining the way you do? How do you know to talk to your children like that? Why does it look like you're having fun parenting?"

I quickly realized that there was a disconnect somewhere. Why weren't our friends asking their parents or siblings about how to raise children? Why were we, a young couple who really had no idea what we were doing, being asked all these questions? After much thought and conversation, I discovered that the disconnect was within families, and it wasn't specific to Australia. My friends didn't feel quite enough when it came to parenting, and they didn't feel they could ask their parents about it, or maybe they didn't have confidence in their answers. Obviously, they saw something different in the way Philip and I were going about our newfound roles as parents, so the questions rolled in.

This led me to start an organization in 2001 called thefamilyroom. Through thefamilyroom, we hosted live events to gather the community and celebrate family together. We brought businesses together to support women. We worked against the disconnect that was so evident by connecting people.

Then, in the early 2000s, Google started using keywords and phrases, which allowed early adopters of blogging the opportunity to connect in a more in-depth way with others who were seeking the same answers. So whilst I was experiencing the pain of cracked nipples, sleepless nights, hours of soothing croup, declined intimacy with my husband, and increased irritability for both of us, somehow in those hours, my life as a blogger was birthed—all in response to the disconnect I had observed.

In 2005, my first articles were published through a website we had created. It was exciting. I wrote about the great things that were happening in my life as I was raising kids, keeping a marriage together, working, and trying to juggle everything. I also told the truth about the terrible and painful days.

Contrasting my style of blogging, conversations about women being "superwomen" were floating about during this time, and everyone was seemingly buying into this awful story of "we can do and have it all." Meanwhile, at home they were crumbling under the pressure of having to have and do it all and look beautiful in the process—the perfect body, the home that could rival the cover of any interior design magazine, and the well-behaved children. And this was before Instagram! Just thinking about superwomen exhausted and frustrated me. It was a culture that bred the message: You aren't enough, and you never will be.

That message added meaning to the dialog I was having with women through my blog. It set a context for when I blogged about the good days, the downright awful days, the stuff that was stressing me out, the times when I felt like a success as a parent, and then the times that I felt like an absolute failure and totally missed it. Now, fast-forward through twenty years of parenting, and there are still times when I feel like a complete failure, and I continue to write about it.

My Message to You

One of these times came almost two years ago while I was sitting at my daughter Sophia's high school graduation ceremony. I recall watching her walk down the aisle of the gymnasium. She was poised and beautiful. My mind quickly flashed back to the first day I drove her to prep school all those years ago. Perched in her booster seat with her lunch box clenched in her hand, a look of excitement covering what I could tell was a touch of four-year-old angst, we made our way through the streets to Discovery House, where she would spend the next few years learning and exploring. It was the beginning of her independence. This, her graduation day, was another huge step toward independence.

Although I could talk about all her successes and all her accomplishments, as I watched her, what flooded my mind in that moment was an overwhelming sense of being alone. It wasn't the memories of the successes and all the things I had done right or the moments that have been fantastic that stood out to me. Instead, I looked at my failures, and the times that I didn't make it.

Why is it that as twenty-first-century women who have walked through so many challenges and risen from them we *still* go to that dark place in our minds? Why do we dwell on what we consider to be our failures? Having heard from women all over the world for the last twenty years, I can guess with great confidence that you, like most women, struggle with this same challenge, at least from time to time.

If this is something you have ever dealt with in your life, please hear my message to you today: I want you to know that you matter. I see you, I know you, and I'm with you. You aren't a mistake, and you aren't an embarrassment. You are beautiful —even your lumpy bits, your bony bits, your fragile bits, and your crazy bits. You are a carrier of light, and you are simply amazing.

This is where I want to start. I want you to know from the beginning that you are magnificent, and you are seen. You are these things because this is how God made you, and God never changed his mind about you. Your story matters, and your journey through life thus far—perhaps challenging, disappointing, and painful, and perhaps seasoned with joy, laughter, and friendship—all matters.

I'm sure you, like me, have had times when you have roared, times when you have bled, and times when you have shed tears that no one has seen. You aren't alone; we've all been there. I wholeheartedly believe that within each one of us there is greatness, and through some of the messiest and most challenging times, there is gold. There is beauty to be restored, and some that is yet to be seen.

I also believe that as a clan and more so as part of our humanity, it is incumbent upon all of us to look and see the beauty that we all possess. We need to recognize the dignity we have in being created in God's image—the thing that connects us to each other, to the planet, and most importantly to God—our Creator, and the Creator of the universe.

Maybe for you, God is the one in this list to whom you feel least connected, or to whom you want to be least connected. I can only tell you that it's through my connection to God that I've come to understand that my connectedness to everything else is greater than I ever imagined.

After taking time to journey inward and making a conscious decision to quiet my heart, mind, and soul, I have found that our connectedness is deep and rich, where the distraction of my very self is diminished. I'm so grateful I responded to the call from within urging me to quiet myself, so I could hear. Connectedness is made real through the hundreds of hours of conversations I had with women across the globe—stories of lives lived, and truths shared; stories that tie us to one another, stories that change the way we see one another, which translates into the way we treat each other.

As you begin to read this, may I boldly suggest that together we let go and let God. Let's open ourselves up for a deep work that is rich and transformational. We need to give ourselves and others the freedom and permission to simply be—be us, undressed and naked, yet turned to the light, no longer afraid of our pain, no longer hiding in the shadows of shame and guilt but prepared to share our truth, so that others may also find the strength to be who they are meant to be. Through our truth, may we be a light that leads others to live in freedom.

I wholeheartedly believe that although life can feel hard, life in itself is beautiful. The struggles and challenges in life can be difficult, but when we take all that away, and life stands alone, it's simply beautiful—beautiful because it's life, bursting with color and experiences waiting for us, adventures to be had, and fullness that God desires for us—more than we can imagine.

Showing up is sometimes the hardest part of this. It takes courage to show up. You may be sliding into home plate frayed, confused, and dazed, or maybe you glided across first, second, and third base with bra straps in place and hair and nails on point. Whatever your case may be, I think of the words crafted by Brené Brown in her "Manifesto of The Brave and the Brokenhearted," where she says, "Showing up is our power. Story is our way home. Truth is our song. We are the brave and brokenhearted."[1]

Those words resonate with me. I feel like the brave and the brokenhearted. I feel like a woman who has shown up regardless of circumstance or situation. I have hiked up my big girl panties and danced (sometimes stumbled) through life—because when the truth is out, and when you see God with you, you can walk through anything.

YOU ARE MORE

You are more. More than your thoughts, emotions.
More than your hopes and dreams
More than your work and position
More than the passage of time in your body
More than your failures and shortcomings
More than your accomplishments and possessions
More than your partner, children, or parents
More than the dysfunction of your family of origin
More than the words with which you label yourself
More than the facts that support them
More than the lies you keep in your heart
More than the grief you have endured
More than the abuse you have suffered
More than the hurts inflicted on you, that you inflicted on
yourself and others
More than the voice that keeps you down
You are more.
You are more than yourself.
You are more than enough.

1

IF THE TRUTH SETS YOU FREE, WHY AM I STUCK IN LIES?

A lie can travel halfway around the world while the truth is putting on its shoes.

—CHARLES SPURGEON[2]

The bathroom floor was cold and felt damp beneath me as I slumped over the toilet. The house was bursting with guests. Relatives from overseas had come for a holiday, and my new husband and I were living in Hong Kong, which meant high rent and tight quarters. With space made for guests, the only place I could go to be alone was the bathroom. I gently pulled the lid of the toilet down, cushioned my head in the crook of my arm, and sobbed.

We had just celebrated the perfect wedding, which is still talked about to this day. To those who knew us, we were a vibrant couple who seemed to have it all. We had great careers and took extraordinary holidays. Life seemed as if it was dusted with magic. But draped over the toilet in the dark, I curled in sadness. The pains of heartache, broken promises, and shattered dreams overcame me, and we were not even a year into our marriage. The pain was real, and this was my truth.

We were living in lies, sweeping our problems under the carpet, and blazing forward with life. The hidden secret of our pain was crippling, but it stemmed from things we had brought into our marriage—the things that had not been dealt with: poor choices, addictions, and so much more. Like many, we lived a lie and believed if anyone knew our truth, pain, and what we were walking through, we would lose it all: friends, marriage, roles in church … it would all disappear. The scorn and sadly, the judgment seemed too much to bear. Living the lie seemed like the more viable answer. Bury it, keep it silent, live in pain, live life with a thin cover of gloss over it all, and you're safe. The option to live free in our truth wasn't an option.

Philip

I met Philip in 1990 while we were both living in Hong Kong. He had grown up there, and I had moved there from Canada after my father was appointed as a diplomat. Fresh-faced and ready to take the world by storm, I packed my suitcase, bid some hard farewells to those I loved and boarded my flight. Now, may I remind you that in 1990, Facebook was nearly two decades away, and Mark Zuckerberg was only six years old. There was, however, the trusty fax machine and exorbitant long-distance charges. My connectivity to home would be limited to weekly phone calls, daily faxes, and good old-fashioned letter writing.

Philip and I met at The Jockey, a British pub where I was working at the time. His friend was interested in me, and Phil came along as his wingman one night. I was instantly attracted to him. He was seemingly flawless with perfect skin, great teeth, and immaculate fashion. He was so well put together and so well spoken. In fact, he had the most delicious English accent, which stemmed from his schooling in Hong Kong where he studied the Queen's English. He had me at hello!

We got married, and like any couple, the dream was one of a happy union filled with fun, laughter, great adventures, and lots of sex. To put it simply, and to my shock, my married life was anything but the dream. At one point, I couldn't stand Philip's laugh or the thought of being intimate, and I'm sure he has felt the same. It was a rough and lonely place, and to be truly authentic, the cracks became evident shortly after our honeymoon.

In truth, we were living a lie. We were covered in stains from our past and plagued with challenges, addictions, and immaturity. We adopted the "fake-it-'til-you-make-it" idea and trudged our way through our everyday lives. I felt trapped, fighting and screaming for release, but my voice was silenced because I bought into the lie that we couldn't let our truth out. We couldn't share it because sometimes people don't want to know. We would have been "those people."

But truthfully, my biggest fear was losing my marriage and the man I had fallen deeply in love with. I was also scared my pride would crumble, and I would have to face the humiliation of failure—as a wife and lover. We had failed to address the messes in our individual lives before starting our life together. I look back now, and my heart breaks for those young kids who had no idea they'd spend the next twenty plus years crawling their way to a place of joy, truth, and vulnerability.

The years have been many, and I have wanted to give up many times when I felt I had seriously had enough. But as we have bravely lifted the lid off our "stuff" (and I promise you, there has been a lot), we have risen strong—together. We have allowed ourselves to be brave and broken. We looked at the mountain ahead of us, laced up our boots, and together we climbed—tear by tear and angry word by angry word. Naked, we chose to turn to the light, which burned away the garbage. We have found ourselves, and we stand in our truth.

It's been hard; like life, it has been filled with both light and shadow. But it's been so worth it, and through it all, both of us have kept at least one foot pointing toward each other. For that, I'm filled with gratitude.

In Silence We Find Truth: The Transformation

What does light look like? For us, it finally came in the form of silence, quiet, meditation, and a deep desire to connect with ourselves and one another in a way that we'd never experienced. We turned to God, but not in the hand-raising, happy-clappy, begging-prayer way that we had practiced for most of our lives. Rather, we sat quietly in the presence of God—in the presence of love. We became still and silent, so that we could hear and be rather than talk and do. We asked ourselves, *What had talking really done for us? What had doing and striving done?* Nothing. It was time to change strategies and try something outside of our normal.

We also had a great community around us. We took stock of the friends we had, set boundaries, made changes, and embraced the community that walked with us. We also had professional help from Paul, our very skilled therapist who has seen and heard the worst and best of us. For those of you who hesitate at the thought of therapy, I strongly urge you to reconsider. If you had cancer, you would see an oncologist. God gave us doctors as a gift. For us, seeing Paul has been one of the wisest decisions we have made in the past twenty-plus years together.

Throughout our trials, we've surprised ourselves with how strong we are—as a couple and as individuals. As for myself, I've heard it said that you don't really know strength until you meet a woman who has rebuilt herself, which is something I have come to know and believe without a shadow of a doubt. Through our pain, hurt, and sadness, we've found and discovered us. We love deeper, we trust in new ways, and we see life through a more beautiful lens—a lens that allows us to see God within each other, and in that we find healing in surprising places. We are peeled back, raw and exposed, and it's in that truth that we inhale and exhale. I know through my own lived experience that when our truth is out, we can walk through anything.

Have you ever had the experience of holding onto something that isn't true? You've denied the reality, but then when you finally speak it, it's like the pressure is released, and the lies you allowed yourself to believe are extinguished. You let go of the fears that whisper, *What if they find out? Will they still like me? Will I be kicked out? Will they look at me differently when they know my truth?*

I'm not naïve. Some may look at me differently for sharing the truth of the mess I've lived in, but who cares? I'm all about linking arms with women and people who have broken their "give-a-darn" button and who see and hear you through their own story, instead of through the arbitrary standard culture forces on us.

What a beautiful way to be known—through truth. We must no longer sacrifice "self" to appease others and to fit in. When we choose to fit in with others, we no longer fit ourselves, and that cost is too great. It trades who God made us to be with who society says we should be, and it forces us into a silence that bars us from healing.

I've seen the ways that I've made this very sacrifice in the past and have decided to no longer operate that way. Rather, I choose to be fully myself. The outcome of living true to yourself is incredible freedom, and it's something I hope all of us can experience. You being yourself is enough.

There is beauty in ashes. There is beauty in pain. There is beauty in the story of you. In your story of truth, there is a girl who once believed in white picket fences, the tooth fairy, and who perhaps even thought the birds around Cinderella's head were real. Maybe you were a girl who dreamed a knight in shining armor would ride in on a strong steed and save her from the castle that kept her hidden.

Alas, the fairytale didn't happen, and the white picket fence may look more like an unkempt hedge. The tooth fairy is and always was your mother or father, and as you've moved through life and battled a few raging storms, you've learned that the birds around Cinderella's head are just one-dimensional images in a storybook. Everyone knows that your knight in shining armor is flawed. He won't always save you, and maybe he hasn't even protected you like you thought he would.

We live in the real world where stories are lived, and tales are told. We need to start flourishing in reality—one breath and non-negotiated moment at a time. Yes, this also means in church-world. Christians are by no means exempt from pulling up the curtains to maintain the image that everything's perfect; in fact, they're probably better at it than the non-Christian world.

We think life with God is supposed to be clean and tidy. It's not. God is a redeemer and healer. If we don't have mess, what does God redeem? If we don't have pain, what does God heal? Just because God's in your life doesn't mean it's perfect; it just means there's hope for something better. But we first have to be honest with ourselves about the things in our lives that need to change. When we stop wasting time by hiding the truth and instead embrace it—regardless of how ugly it may look or how tough it may be—we begin to find freedom.

Kill the Lies, Walk in Freedom: Helen's Story

I recently hosted a retreat, and we did an exercise where each woman wrote down something she wanted to let go of. Then they read it aloud and burned it in the fire. This is Helen's heartfelt story.

Helen spoke of her father and the pain she experienced as a young girl when she heard him verbally abusing her mother.

Helen described her father as "a street angel and a house devil." On some nights, the abuse was physical. As a little girl, she remembered trying to shield her mother when his words moved to punches, when he pulled her hair, and when he shoved her. She had seen enough to know that each punch, each push, and each time he slammed her face into the wall or tabletop could be the last.

Her mother was a kind woman. She was timid, but Helen watched her mother transform into a strong woman who became and remains her hero today. Finally, when Helen was eighteen, her father left for good after a night of beating. Leaving the two of them for dead, he left them with no money and no support—just scars and a memory of a once-loved father.

Through tears, she shared her story and her inability to forgive him. She spoke of her profound understanding that unforgiveness, anger, and feelings of abandonment were holding her back in life. Unforgiveness was suffocating her, like a weight around her ankles that wouldn't allow her to move forward.

There she stood, fifty years old, surrounded by people she had only just met, and she was sharing her truth. She had been empowered to name it, speak it out, and make peace with the pain so that she could move forward. She was letting the truth out. She trusted the process we had created and the explanation of how the lies we believe about ourselves can hold us back.

She spoke with courage as she looked into the flames and said, "When you left, I was lost. I was hurt, and I questioned whether I was lovable. I only knew the things you told me—the times you told me I was worthless, that I was a mistake, and that I would never, ever become anything, that I was taking up space. Those words were lies because I am lovable, and I'm loved, and I love. I am not worthless, and I was never a mistake. The only mistake was the way you chose to live, and the way you decided to treat those who loved you unconditionally. And, yes, I do take up space, and it's valuable space. I forgive you, and tonight

I throw these words and the lies I've believed into this fire. To-night, I'm choosing to live a life of freedom, no longer bound by the pain of the past or the words that have played over and over in my mind. I am free."

With that, she threw the letter she had written into the fire, and the women who were with her cheered for her and wept tears of joy. They knew it was her time to walk in freedom—free of the pain that had held her captive.

Why am I compelled to help women kill the lies we've believed about ourselves? It's because I know that as we walk in our own freedom, we give permission for others to do the same. As we bravely confess that we are the brave and the brokenhearted, that life has dealt us some wrong hands, we can still rise.

The lies we believe trap us and pull us away from the realities of our authentic selves. We become distant from the women who God created to live with intent and to impact the earth. When we live through lies instead of living with intention, we aimlessly wander and roam. We search for meaning and belonging, and instead of walking in community, we walk alone. We chase down paths we think may lead us to a sense of belonging when the journey we need to take is the one that allows our hearts and minds to connect. It is when we surrender to God that we are able to rebuild from the inside out, giving us the strength to take this pilgrimage together toward our true selves.

Reclaim Power: Louise's Story

In her forties as a single mother of one child, Louise felt her life had stopped in her early twenties. She shared with me about her inability to move forward in life, and she told me about a friend from her younger years whom she had always admired. In her mind, this friend had everything together, and Louise desired her approval.

Throughout life, Louise constantly found herself wondering

When I stop believing lies, I will find freedom to be "me".

what that friend would think of the decisions she was making. Instead of limiting her curiosity to a fleeting thought, she allowed it to fester. She held onto the lie that what this person thought of her mattered, even now that she was in her forties. As Louise verbalized this, it was almost as if the lights began to turn on.

I asked her a simple question: "You seem to think of this person a lot. She seems to weigh in on your decisions almost daily. How often do you think she thinks of you and wonders what you would think of her life choices?"

Tears rolled down her face. She started to recognize the utter ridiculousness of the situation. She had given this woman so much power, and it significantly impacted her life. Slowly, Louise composed herself and replied, "I don't think she would think of me at all."

Our conversation changed after that. We started to speak the truth of who Louise is as a person and why she didn't need to consider this other woman from her past. We talked about how this woman's words and ideas about her life were of no significance and would no longer impact Louise and the life she was meant to live.

As we spoke these words out loud, she declared the truth and reclaimed the power over her life. The opinions of people from her past, present, and future do not and will not change who she is. By killing the lies and embracing the truth, we walk in freedom. Sometimes it's as simple as naming the lie, speaking it out, and taking the power back. By bravely facing the light, naked and unashamed, through tears and ugly cries, we take back what is ours. It's a beautiful thing.

Once we replace lies with the truth, we begin to stand on solid ground rather than quicksand. As we let go and let God, we truly embark on a journey of life, healing, and wholeness, a life that can only be discovered through surrendering our will to something bigger than our own understanding. Submitting to something greater than ourselves allows something restorative to happen.

It starts by taking a good look at ourselves from the inside out, verbalizing and taking responsibility for our wrongs, and surrendering to God so that we make way for Him to do deep work within us. We come before God to ask for the shortcomings in our lives to be removed, then we can address the people in our lives whom we have wronged and do whatever we can to make it right. We use ongoing prayer and meditation to connect to God in a meaningful way, and from this place of freedom, we welcome others into the same experience. Our job is not only finding a way to freedom for ourselves, but it's also walking step by step with others to help them become free too.

We Stand on the Shoulders of Giants

After we recognize the lies we have believed and lived, we need to think about those who have been impacted by them as we have limped our way through life. I think of my children. I want them to know that Philip and I have been brave enough to face our truth, so that they may live even stronger.

There is a seventeenth century concept that says we are "standing on the shoulders of giants." This concept is perhaps most famously attributed to pioneering scientist Isaac Newton, who wrote in a letter dated in 1675 to his rival Robert Hooke, "What Descartes did was a good step. You have added much several ways, and especially in taking the colors of thin plates into philosophical consideration. If I have seen a little further, it is by standing on the shoulders of giants."

This phrase has since been attributed to earlier sources than Newton. As early as the twelfth century, theologian and author John of Salisbury referenced this phrase. Oh, how great ideas flow and are shared by such minds! In his work, *Metalogicon*, written in Latin in 1159, he elaborates:

> We frequently know more, not because
> we have moved ahead by our own natu-
> ral ability, but because we are supported
> by the [mental] strength of others, and
> possess riches that we have inherited from
> our forefathers. Bernard of Chartres used
> to compare us to [puny] dwarfs perched
> on the shoulders of giants. He pointed
> out that we see more and farther than our
> predecessors, not because we have keener
> vision or greater height, but because we
> are lifted up and borne aloft their gigantic
> stature.[3]

This idea of learning from and expanding on the beliefs and concepts of others is why I truly believe communities flourish when we gather and collaborate—because when we push each other higher, we can soar. I believe that I stand on the shoulders of giants. When I look throughout my family history, I see that I come from a line of strong women and men who paved a way for me. This compels me to live freely in the hope that my children and others will live beyond my limits.

Our children can stand on our shoulders, but this means we have to be honest and vulnerable with them about our truth. Many of us who have children have heard it said that you shouldn't fight in front of them. We shouldn't let them into our business; they should be protected from the grime of life. This may be ideal, but it's not often the reality. The question is how we should handle the truth of our public conflicts. Do we act like they never happened? What does that teach our children? What would it teach them if instead we were honest about the fact that spouses argue sometimes? What if we showed our children that despite arguments, we still work to come together and strengthen our marriages?

If you consider what Salisbury said, perhaps our children will live more strongly, understand more, have more compassion, and love more deeply because they stand on our shoulders and on our truth. And if you include Brené Brown's discovery that vulnerability is the key to connection in relationships, then we have to recognize that taking ownership of our truth is a necessary part of offering shoulders for others to stand on.

Perhaps the idea that shielding and protecting our children from the mess of life has its limits. Perhaps there is an age where they can manage the messy realities of life. What if their lived experience is rich with wisdom and knowledge because they have seen the pain, hardship, angst, and sorrow, and because of that, they are stronger? Not just because they have seen these things, but because they have witnessed us endure such trials and come out the other side even stronger.

Sophia

Our eldest daughter, Sophia, has seen much of our ugly. We tried to keep her out of our mess, but being an inquisitive child, she involved herself by reading our text messages and nosing into everything. She left no stone unturned and then crafted her own narrative as to what was happening in our marriage. Now, at twenty, she is still unpacking what she had determined was truth, which is a far cry from what was.

In fact, she told me about a something she'd first believed when she was twelve. It started with an episode of Dr. Phil we had watched together. The show was about domestic abuse and how to plan your escape if you are in this situation (honestly, the show was amazing, and I do recommend a Google search of the archived episode if you are in a dangerous situation). Dr. Phil explained the need for cash when fleeing an abusive family situation and encouraged the abused partner to have a significant amount of cash on hand when leaving the relationship.

We went on a vacation to visit family about six weeks after we had watched Dr. Phil's show. Sophia knew that Philip and I were having trouble. She and her cousins asked if they could have some money to go to the corner store for ice cream. I told them to grab some money from my wallet, which was a normal thing in our home. Sophia opened my wallet and saw that I had a lot of cash, which was unusual for me. Sophia's narrative started to develop.

Her young mind had pieced together our challenges, the Dr. Phil show, and the cash and concluded that Philip and I were done. My sweet girl! I can only imagine the anxiety she must have felt, and the wavering sense of security she experienced. She went through all of this because we had done everything we could to shelter her from our truth. You can see how poorly that worked out.

She's a young adult now, and she only just told me about all of this. Her lived experience was rooted in lies. Sure, we were having trouble, but not to the extent she had determined in her mind, and certainly not to the extent where I needed to heed the advice from Dr. Phil's show. The truth has now set her free, but how my heart as a mother aches because my sweet girl sat cloaked in fear for years because we had concealed the truth. Our vulnerability could have set her free.

This was the experience that broke us. We had brought our pain, lies, deception, and ugly into her life despite our attempts to protect her from it all. We realized that our immaturity, lack of self-discipline, and unwillingness to face the truth created a situation where our daughter found herself having to piece it together on her own. The pain was unbearable for both of us, and we consider this time one of our lowest points on our journey thus far.

Sophia's name means wisdom, and she does her name proud. She has come through this with wisdom beyond her years. She is someone I aspire to be like. She sees beyond the layer of gloss that people often show, and she loves deeply.

We, however, had been caught up in our lies, which were choking the life out of us. We faced the reality of our truth to show our precious daughter that restoration is real. We needed to be authentic and true, not only for ourselves but also for her and for all our children. We needed to be the shoulders they could stand on.

Was it easy? No, not at all. Was it scary? Absolutely. We had become so comfortable and so skilled (or so we thought) at living in the lie that facing the truth and choosing to turn to the light, naked and brave, was not only humbling but also painful. I was scared. Forget that; I was terrified.

Did we make it? Where did we land? Well, read on, dear friend, because my hope is that as you do, you will find yourself within these pages—in the stories people have shared with me, or perhaps through my own story. I hope you will link arms with me and countless others, and together we will bravely and boldly make it.

May our stories become rich broth that nourishes your soul. May they give life and transform us from the inside out.

A Practice from The Gathering Cloud
Retreating to Address Lies Others Have Said

[handwritten margin notes: dad treating me like im stupid. telling me I make poor decisions. my family, when they joke about me being "special". the boys that have told me "they just don't see me that way". I am insecure about my intelligence.]

1. Take a moment to consider the lies others have said you have believed. Is there someone in your past who has spoken words over you that have taken up residence in your heart? Do those words jump out at you whenever you want to make a change? Maybe these words tell you "You can't," or "You're not smart enough," or maybe they remind you of past failures. Maybe someone in your life is projecting their lies onto you and keeping you down to feel better about themselves. What comes to mind when you ask yourself these questions?

2. Write down the lies that come to you.

3. Invite the Holy Spirit to rest in your thoughts and emotions: "Spirit of Truth, speak your truth to me."

[handwritten margin note: I have a mind that God wants to use for good.]

4. Recall a lie you have believed from someone else. Acknowledge it as a lie and then speak what is true. For example, if someone has said you are stupid, the truth is that you have a mind God wants to use for good. Repeat the truth to yourself and let that lie go.

5. Repeat this until you want to stop.

[handwritten:]
I have a mind that God wants to use for good.
I have a mind that God wants to use for good.
I have a mind that God wants to use for good.
I have a mind that God wants to use for good.
I have a mind that God wants to use for good.
I am so smart, and have special skills that God can use for good.

2

THE SPIN CYCLE

Have you ever found yourself scrolling through social media feeds, and as you scroll, you see countless photos of the seemingly perfect life? Everything is in its perfect position. The kitchens are clean, the cars are clean, the freshly baked goodies are housed in glass containers, the birthday parties are perfectly decorated, the kids are well dressed with combed hair, and their clothing is on point—down to the tuck of the shirt. It's the perfect, happy family. It's seriously insane some days.

Welcome to the Spin Cycle! As a mother of three children, I find that I spend a good portion of my time in the laundry room. I seem to get it all cleaned up, and then *bam*! It's crazy and uncontrollable yet again. The lessons I've learned from the laundry are:

1. It will never end. The pile will always grow, and just when you think you're on top of it … it's all back again.

2. The spin cycle is like waiting for a pot of water to boil. When you watch and wait, all it does is spin, spin, and spin some more.

3. The Spin Cycle of what we see in social media is much the same; it seems to go on and on and on. By that I'm referring to two things:

4. We keep spinning around in circles. We get stuck in our lies, and we don't face the truth, so we keep dealing with the same issues in life. Then we only post our shiny moments and highlights.

5. We put a spin on life. If our life is out of control, and the wheels are falling off, we give the impression that everything is lovely; our homes are peaceful, and life is grand. We spin the story, and we insert ourselves into this spin, which puts undue pressure on everyone involved.

Imagine if instead we chose to interrupt the Spin Cycle and speak our truth—to let someone know where we *actually* are in life. What if we stop the lies on social media? I'm not suggesting you post every down and out situation, but what if we chose to be honest about whatever it is we are dealing with—the good *and* the bad?

If all of us did even this much, we would see remarkable change. We would no longer be inserted into this spin cycle. Instead, we would own our truth and allow that to propel us forward. Even more, what if we allowed ourselves to lament when things have gone wrong? What would happen if we gave ourselves permission to address the pain in our lives?

Getting Help

Philip and I decided it was time we addressed our pain, and it's how we found ourselves sitting in the office of our therapist, Paul. We had an upcoming wedding anniversary to celebrate, which served as the catalyst for our decision to seek help since I use the word *celebrate* very loosely.

I don't want to give the impression that our marriage has always been bad. Like so much in life, our marriage has been a combination of light and shadow, with just enough light to keep us from acknowledging the painful, unresolved shadows.

Our anniversary was looming, and Philip always takes it upon himself to organize something beautiful to celebrate our special day. He is the master planner and a romantic. But this year, I wasn't feeling it. There was tension between us. Philip had developed some anger issues, and my response to his anger issues only made things worse. You can only imagine the lack of peace we had in our house.

I took a good, hard look at our lives. I realized I was living in tension, frustration, and pain. We had recently had a major fight, and in my mind, our marriage wasn't much to celebrate. He had done the obligatory booking of the hotel and planning a beautiful dinner, which was our usual celebration. It would have been a lovely time out; the Instagram and Facebook posts would have been amazing. Hidden beneath the perfectly curated shot, however, would have been a couple in pain.

I decided I wasn't going. Once again, we were hobbling through life—too stubborn or too foolish to address the elephant in the room. We were caught in the spin cycle. It was an ugly and painful way to live. I was becoming a shell of who I knew I was meant to be. I was living in a way that denied the person who God made me to be, yet I was dangerously comfortable because it was familiar. I needed out.

First, I told Philip I wasn't going on our romantic getaway. I told him I felt we currently had nothing to celebrate, and I needed to stop pretending things were fine. Secondly, I suggested he take some time alone and use that time to think. While he was away, I sent him an email with a subject line that read, *Our therapy session is booked. Put the date in your diary. We're going.* The body of the email read, *Happy Anniversary. I hope you're enjoying yourself.*

I admit it was probably a little harsh, but I felt we needed to get real—and fast. We needed to get out of the spin cycle and deal with our issues head on. Therapy sounded liberating to me. I was so excited to sit down with our therapist and throw everything onto the table. I didn't realize how long I had been holding onto pain, thinking I had dealt with things only to realize I had been carrying my hurt with me all along. I had been allowing myself and my family to be sucked into the spin cycle.

Even simply recognizing our need to acknowledge and deal with our pain was a huge first step. Some cultures are remarkably proactive about this, and we can learn from their example. The Jewish calendar includes a day called Tisha B'Av, and it is regarded as the saddest day of the year. On this day, Jewish people mourn and lament the tragedies and pain their people have suffered. I find this an exceptional thing to do. It is so real, so intentional, and ultimately, so freeing to set aside a day to lament the pain we've experienced—to address it rather than place it in the spin cycle. That was what I was trying to do with my husband. I was trying to find a place where we could properly lament and grieve the hurts we had carried, so that we could find healing from them and build the marriage we wanted.

The Real You: Donna's Story

I have heard countless stories over the years of women who feel stuck in the spin cycle. One of the most powerful ones that has stuck with me is Donna's story. Donna was the youngest of a large family, and ever since she made a few wrong moves, she had been labelled the "naughty one." She had become the butt of jokes within the family, and people had all but given up on her because they expected she would mess up anyway.

After years of this treatment from her family, Donna decided to live up to their expectations. She allowed herself to become unruly, reckless, and everything her family thought she was. She allowed herself to get tangled up in destructive relationships. She drank and partied, which led to unplanned pregnancies and a rape that no one in her family knows about to this day. Donna put herself in a different type of spin cycle than Philip and I. Her spin cycle was one in which she had been told who she was for so long that rather than try to prove them wrong, she became who they said she was. How would she jump out of the cycle?

Through tears, she told me that no one knew the real her. She longed to live a life that was true to her authentic self but had no idea of how to do it. She didn't blame her family, but there was a sadness and a desire for them to see her and know her. She cried, "I wish they could see me. I wish they had the opportunity to meet the real me—that I could just show up and be myself."

She told me that the only times she is able to be her authentic self is with a few friends who truly see her and know her to be kind, compassionate, funny, and heartfelt. It's in these friendships that she can step out of the box her family has stuck her in and taste freedom. These friendships help her separate the truth of who she is from the lies she's been told about who she is.

I think of Donna often and would like to wrap my arms around her. I wonder if we met again if she would leave that crack open, the one she created when she shared her story. Would she let me in? Would she be brave enough to link arms with me and share her truth with her family? My prayer is that one day Donna can be her real self with her family and escape the spin cycle. I think the real her would shock them. They would be amazed to know that Donna is an incredible woman who feels and thinks deeply and has silently walked through life hidden, and she has emerged with grace and dignity as their daughter, sister, aunt, and cousin.

Her story is one that will stay with me forever, and she may never know how her truth changed me. Her truth and her story have taught me to parent differently, to listen and learn who my children really are and to help them be fully themselves.

Create a Space for Authenticity: Beth's Story

Another profound moment for me in understanding the spin cycle came years ago as a single, twenty-year-old, brand-new Christian in Hong Kong. I attended a group for women, but I did not fit in at all. I can only think that I went because I didn't know where else to go.

We sat in a circle, and woman by woman we shared about our weeks. Everyone seemed to have days filled with daisies and freshly baked bread. Their ironing was done, their laundry put away, and their cars cleaned. Everything was great, and life was seemingly rolling along to the tune of "Happy Days."

I remember sitting there thinking that this couldn't be true. Of the fifteen people in the room, surely someone had an off week or some challenge. I certainly had. I had nursed a dreadful hangover earlier in the week, and I had a major fight with my boyfriend (now husband). My boss was on my back because he caught me sleeping at work while pretending to do some filing. My week was awful, but because of all the fluff I heard, I thought I would keep my mouth shut rather that burst out what I really wanted to say.

Aside from my own issues at the time, the Gulf War was going on, and a massive sense of uncertainty was disturbing the world. My personal existence was not unlike the state of the world, yet these women seemed unscathed. I was astonished by this level of perfection. I struggled to believe that all was so good, especially since I knew some of these women had teenage children. Knowing how I was as a teenager, I knew one of them surely must have been having trouble with parenting. But no, every week the conversation was the same: perfect, perfect, perfect.

And then it happened: The "aha" moment that changed my life and has stayed with me and propelled me to dig deeper and listen closer: In walked Beth. Beth was late for the meeting, and from the moment her presence was known, I knew something was up. She came in, sat down, and slouched in her chair. She graciously said hello, apologized for her lateness, and asked that we carry on.

We had moved to the ninth woman in the circle who told of another perfect week full of daisies, fresh bread, clean toilets, and all things yummy. Ten. Eleven. Twelve. All the way to Beth, and it was finally her turn. She straightened up in her chair, brushed her hair aside and said, "Well, you've all had wonderful weeks. Mine has been terrible, I'm crabby (she actually swore, but I'm using this word as a placeholder), and I have a bad attitude."

I almost jumped out of my seat and punched my fist into the air. I wanted to yell, "Thank you for not filling us with fluff! Thank you for being honest! Thank you for sharing your truth! Thank you for letting this twenty-year-old know that authenticity is real! Thank you for validating every thought in my mind! Thank you for being brave enough to be you!"

You'll be happy to know I didn't do any of that. Instead, I listened to that small voice that repeatedly told me to sip a mug of shut-up, and I listened while Beth went where she needed to go. As she spoke, I recall the expressions of shock and horror on the other women's faces. Beth's truth was out, and with that I knew she was able to start her long journey toward her new normal.

As it turned out, her husband was cheating on her, abusing her verbally, and the list went on from there. She was hurting; in fact, she was dying right in front of us for weeks. Sadly, the space to be real hadn't been created, so she suffered in silence until she could no longer take it.

Imagine if a space had been created for Beth to be honest. Imagine if Beth had been able to speak her truth before getting to that dead-end road lacking vision and hope. Imagine if things had been different. What if her truth had been known before her pain became so great?

how do we create the space for authenticity?

Let's Be Real

After hundreds of conversations with women from across the globe, I have discovered that not much has changed when it comes to sharing authenticity. Although we think things have changed, not much has shifted since the days when I sat with those women in Hong Kong and listened to their same varnished stories week after week.

We talk about living in freedom. We post about it, and thanks to people like Brené Brown, Jen Hatmaker, Glennon Melton Doyle, Lisa Gungor, Sarah Bessy, and Jamie Wright (just to name a few), we are beginning to embrace it. But when truth *is* revealed, are we entirely sure we are willing to walk through the ugly and painful moments that come with it?

Considering all of the conversations I've had, I have to ask the question: Are we prepared to accept and understand that life is hard, scary, and sometimes maybe even unbearable? Because it's in these raw conversations that we can truly begin to live. It's from this point that change can and will happen. To stop the spin cycle, we have to start sharing the truth.

Maybe we are afraid that if we admit to our problems, lies, and pain, it means we'll set up camp there and never leave. That's not what it means. The truth means admitting we have camped and spun in our pain for far too long, and having admitted it, we can propel ourselves into something better.

unbearable

what things do I need to "let out" and talk about with friends?

A Practice from The Gathering Cloud
Retreating to Stop the Spin Cycle

[handwritten: Justification + protection]

[handwritten left margin: ...on't want to ...rden other people. ...raid of what others ...ll think. that my ...iggles are worse than ...irs. afraid ppl will ...ee my me as weak.]

1. Take a moment to consider any lies you yourself have propagated. Why do you think you propagated them? To protect yourself? To protect someone else? To hurt someone else? Because of fear of failure or success? What comes to mind when you ask yourself these questions? *[handwritten: 5]*

[handwritten left margin: no one will care. I am weak. I bring struggles on myself. feel like I need to understand / work thru my emotions before I tell people.]

2. Write down the lies that come to mind. *[handwritten: i make bad decisions.]*

3. Invite the Holy Spirit to come rest in your thoughts and emotions: "Spirit of Truth, speak your truth to me."

[handwritten left margin: im not good enough to be in a healthy relationship.]

4. Recall a lie you have believed and propagated. Acknowledge it as a lie and then speak what is true. Ask God to forgive you for spreading that lie. Repeat the truth to yourself and let that lie go. *[handwritten: im so sorry. ive been believing this lie, lord. it is a disgrace to who you made me to be.]*

[handwritten left margin: should talk to someone about my "dreams". about my struggles w/ art.]

5. Repeat this until you want to stop.

[handwritten:]
I am worthy of a healthy relationship. I am not broken or "too much.

I am worthy of a healthy relationship. I am not broken or "too much".

I am worthy of a healthy relationship with myself.

I am worthy of a healthy relationship with the Lord.

I am worthy of healthy and life-giving friendships. I am not broken or "too much".

I am wise & capable of making good decisions.
I am wise & capable of making good decisions.

3

WHY DO I FEEL ALONE IN A HYPER-CONNECTED WORLD?

*Loneliness and the feeling of being unwanted
is the most terrible poverty.*

—MOTHER TERESA

We live in a hyper-connected world. We are more connected than we have ever been. I think back to my sweet Nana who came across the ocean from Scotland to Canada. As a little girl, she boarded a big ship with her family. Most of them made it to Canada, but sadly, some died along the way. She was raised in this new land, set up home, and raised a family of her own.

I think of her sitting in her rocking chair and telling us stories of her family. I think of how long she used to have to wait for letters to receive news from home. I think of how lonely she must have been; this little girl who came across the sea and left everything she knew to set up home in Canada amongst strangers.

Fast forward to today and our reliance on instant connectivity. We can see what someone else is doing in an instant. We jump on Facebook, Instagram, Twitter, or Snapchat, and we see what our friend ate for lunch. We can Facetime our family from opposite sides of the planet. We can be present in rooms without physically being there. As a society, we are more connected than ever, but as individuals, we are lonelier than ever before. What is the disconnect?

Loneliness—Connected, yet Desperately Disconnected

I have spoken to so many women who said that loneliness is their biggest challenge. We're sitting in our homes, lounging on our couches, lying in our beds, scrolling through Facebook, Instagram, or whatever social space we prefer, and we're looking at people's highlights and comparing them to our lowlights.

Comparison is a killer, but what is comparison anyway? At its core, comparison tries to establish levels and differences. It focuses on the notion that I'm better, or you're better, but no one wins. We are just left with discontentment.

What we're faced with now is a population of people who sit around comparing themselves to others. We're comparing our messy laundry rooms with the immaculate show-home we've landed on in a feed. Perhaps it's the home of a friend, or it could even be the home of a total stranger. We are comparing our cooking and the way our kids behave and dress. And now we don't stop at the photo; we watch behind the scenes through Instagram stories, Snapchat, and Facebook Live.

We listen and look for anything out of place and admire those sponsored shots, but some of us are searching for sneaky signs of product placement. We allow ourselves to be bombarded by lives we don't live, by highlights reels that are just that: highlights. We forget that everyone has their lowlights.

All of this constant comparison feeds the loneliness and disconnection that we are experiencing. It's almost like a drug. We scroll and scrutinize, desperate to feel good about ourselves, but it has the opposite effect. It eats up time, and we start letting things slide at home that we wouldn't ordinarily let slide. We are absorbed and lost in a world that feeds every possible insecurity—the party you weren't invited to, the holiday you cannot afford, the body that is not yours ... it's endless.

Perfect Posts for Self-Preservation: Sarah's Story

On the flip side of all of this is an interesting story shared with me by Şarah, a young, stunning mother of two. Married to the man she met as a teenager, then add a few pets, careers, and international moves, and it's a life that many of us dream of.

Sarah shared about her life and her husband who was walking through the depths of depression. Coupled with other challenges, they were in a position that was far from the love, companionship, and true joy of family she once knew. This surprised me because I had been scrolling through her social media posts, and to be honest, they typically made me feel like a failure as a mother, homemaker, and friend. Her posts were filled with magazine-like images that left my mismatched birthday wrapping paper and masking tape for dust. Her table settings rivaled those of any interior designer, and from what I saw of her posts, her life looked like a dream. Compared to hers, my life looked more like a scene out of *The Addams Family*.

Sarah changed my perspective on social media posts, connectedness, and disconnection. Beneath the shine and perfection of her images was a sadness that she hadn't been able to share. In fact, her life felt like it was crumbling, and for her, the creation of beauty helped preserve her sanity, and her social media platforms were an outlet for that beauty. She gained stability from creating on the outside what wasn't on the inside. Creating beauty brought her joy and connected her to the future she dreamed of. All this allowed her to live through the day-to-day hell she was living.

I don't judge Sarah for what she does to cope. In fact, I slapped myself on the wrist for having judged her in the first place and for allowing myself to go down a path of self-loathing just because my wrapping paper didn't match, and my Christmas tree tilted to the left. I began to look at posts, comments, and conversations very differently. I began to see beneath the shine and gloss. I'm not sure if Sarah knows this, but she was instrumental in helping me decide to embark on writing this book. I'm forever grateful that she trusted me with her truth on that sunny day a few years ago when she chose to show up amidst the pain she was in.

In short, Sarah's story showed me what a trap comparison is. After all, the truth is we never know what a person may be going through that they just aren't showing. We cannot look at their gloss and imagine it to be truly representative of their entire life, or assume they never go through hard times like we do.

For another example of the traps of comparison, just look at the way we compare our children. It's ridiculous for us as parents to compare our children to others. In doing so, we rob our children of allowing them to be fully themselves. I've been guilty of this. I've forced my kids to attend things simply because I knew other kids would. I got this in my head that if they didn't attend, everything would fall apart. What a lie, and what pressure this put on all of us! I recall when the kids were little how we'd compare when they started walking, talking, or playing patty cake, as though these early milestones would have bearing on which children would turn out best as adults. Then, in school, it was grades, sports, and music, and just as useless.

Every parent has their private struggles sometimes, and yes, some more than others. But when I think of all the women's stories I've heard over the years, so many of them were experiencing a personal hell all their own. It was nearly impossible for them to parent perfectly on top of everything else. We see children who may honestly be struggling, but we don't know what their mother or father may be going through behind the scenes. Comparison is never done fairly or equitably, but it riles our emotions anyway; that's how it traps us.

Comparison and Projection: Lisa's Story

I had the opportunity to speak to Lisa about her difficulties with comparing her daughter to other girls. According to Lisa, her daughter falls into the "nerdy" category, so Lisa is desperately concerned for her daughter. By her own admission, Lisa has compared her daughter to the other girls in her class and has even compared her to herself when she was ten. This was dangerous on so many levels. It put unachievable expectations on her daughter, and a pressure to perform in a way she'll never be able to accomplish. I can't imagine the pressure that girl was feeling.

I listened as Lisa told me what she struggled with concerning her daughter. What I found interesting was that all of it was indeed comparison and projection. Lisa asked herself things like, *What if she gets teased? What if she gets left out? What if she gets bullied?* All this projected angst created tension between mother and daughter, which in turn impacted the entire family. I suggested Lisa begin to look at her concerns in a different way. The question wasn't what if she gets teased, bullied, or left out; the question should have been, "What do I do if it happens, and how do I prepare her for those experiences?"

Being a girl, a woman, and now a mother, I've lived long enough to know that girls (and let's be honest, women) can be mean. Lisa needed to take the pressure off her daughter, let her be her fully "nerdy" self, and create a healthy space between them at home where her daughter could find solace when or if those things happened.

It's important to note that I'm not definitively predicting that these things will happen, but if history is a predictor of the future, then we need to understand that our jobs as parents is to create homes that are havens for family and friends. We need to be the light on the hill—the safe place where we become dealers of hope and healing.

Connect or Disconnect?

I've thought a lot about connectedness on a grander scale. What if our connectedness is tied to something bigger than our experiences? We are, by design, deeply connected to one another and the world around us. For example, we need air in our lungs to breathe. Most of the earth's atmospheric oxygen comes from the ocean, and as tides rise and fall in sync with the phases of the moon, we are given breath. Oxygen comes from trees as well, as plants capture sunlight and use its energy to split carbon dioxide and water, which makes sugar and releases oxygen as a byproduct. We use this oxygen to breathe and therefore live, so we can see how connected we are to our environment, or rather, to the earth. Our connectedness goes further than that, however. We are connected to the people around us—we breathe the same air, we walk on the same planet, and we move through life like a well-choreographed dance.

I liken connectedness to circular breathing. If you've ever seen someone play the didgeridoo you will know their mesmerizing ability to circular breathe and stay in flow. Once I pondered our connectedness, I began seeing it everywhere. One great example of it is the Trinity: Father, Son, and Holy Spirit are all individual, yet the same and deeply connected. If you want a resource to dig deeper into this, I like the way Father Richard Rohr describes this connectedness in his book *The Divine Dance*; that title alone captivates my heart.

Our lives are deeply connected in this world that by design

ebbs and flows in unison, so why do we feel so disconnected? How is it that we are so intimately connected, and yet so many of us feel an overwhelming sense of loneliness? I understand it, and I've certainly felt it. When it comes to being disconnected, I think we need to set our minds and hearts on a mission to seek connection with purpose and intention. I think about brands and organizations—even churches that sell these glossy marketing messages about belonging: Sign up to our email list and get this; come to our hotel and fit right in; join our VIP club and get our special deals; come to church and become part of the family. These messages promise connection, but sadly they're the classic cases of over-promising and under-delivering, which compounds our feelings of disconnection.

If we can understand the beauty and truth of our connectedness, we can let go of expectations and simply be. If I have no expectations of what someone will do in my life, then I won't be disappointed and continually look to him or her to fill that need. Instead, understanding our connectedness down to our very breaths relieves tremendous amounts of pressure. Instead of looking to personal connections or organizations to meet all my needs, I understand that I can be connected to a God who will meet all my needs.

I'm Lonely Too: Heathers' Stories

The other night I received a text from a woman named Heather who has attended our GetRealLive Retreats. She asked if we could have a quick chat because she needed to tell me something. I called her, we chatted for a while, and then the flood of tears came.

Through her tears and what I can only describe as an outpouring of intense, painful emotion, she told me how lonely she was. As a single mother with grown daughters making their own ways in life, she explained how deep the pain of loneliness ran.

She said at times her loneliness was even a physical pain that made getting out of bed and going to work a struggle.

My heart broke for her. Instead of providing her with countless examples of how to get involved in her community, the groups she could join, or websites she could visit, I just listened. I let her cry and put it all out there. I sat in her pain with her, listened, and lamented. After she got it out and had a moment to breathe, I whispered, "I'm lonely too." I told her that there are days that I hurt, and I shared my experiences with loneliness— from living far away from family to my children growing up and needing me less. I didn't compare; I sat in the valley with her and let her know that she wasn't alone, her loneliness is real, and it's okay to say it hurts.

I told her the story behind why I do much of what I do. I had read Psalm 68:6 in the Bible, and those words have never left my mind or heart. I remain captivated by this one line which reads, "God sets the lonely in families." With that, I asked her to join us the following Monday night for our family dinner. Sometimes it's as simple as that—sitting with those in pain, empathizing with them, and saying, "You aren't alone. I hear you, I see you, and I'm with you."

During the interviews, I had a conversation with another woman named Heather who shared about her loneliness. Her story is vastly different. She is married with three children, and she loves her life. Her husband is a nice guy, and the family they have built together is her joy. She is the bubbly, active one who is always on the go and volunteering in her community, predominantly at her kid's school and in her church. She seems to be very engaged, and by her admission, she is. Interestingly, she told me that although she is busy and involved, she's never seen.

She's become someone who can be counted on; she's often pulled into a situation and asked to do a lot, but she never feels valued. She sees on social media how the "in-crowd" gets together and socializes after events or projects they all worked on together, and even though she shared in the work, she's never invited to share in the celebration afterward. Instead, she goes home to her family who she loves, but even in that precious cocoon, her loneliness from a lack of friendship and simply from not being included has the potential to drown her.

There is a strange juxtaposition in what this woman is feeling. She is lonely, yet she is surrounded by people. She loves her community but does not feel valued. We often cannot see this type of loneliness from the outside, and that makes it all the more dangerous and heartbreaking. Her story is not unique, but this type of loneliness can be avoided if we choose to look beneath the surface.

Loneliness expresses the pain of being alone
and solitude expresses the glory of being alone.

—Paul Tillich[4]

Loneliness Kills

Many women have tearfully shared with me that they would love someone to give them a call or just ask them for coffee. The lonely ones are usually the people who organize the catch-ups, the dinners, the play dates, etc. Loneliness is so fascinating, but that's not quite the right word. It's not fascinating; it's sad. In fact, Vivek Murthy, the former United States surgeon general, was quoted in an article in the *New York Times* saying that loneliness and social isolation are "associated with a reduction of lifespan similar to that caused by smoking fifteen cigarettes per day and even greater than that associated with obesity."[5] I can't help but think of "Eleanor Rigby," the bleak anthem by the Beatles in which Paul McCartney sings about "all the lonely people." An article in the *Huffington Post* calls loneliness the global epidemic of our times, citing loneliness as "the next big public health issue, on par with obesity, domestic violence, and substance abuse."[6]

We are beginning to recognize that loneliness is a core factor in mental and physical health problems, which means it's something that we need to be aware of. We are social creatures who are designed to be in relationships, so when we're not active with people, we begin to crumble. We are designed to be in emotional, face-to-face, physical relationships, and this disconnect is eroding us.

If you think back to me sitting at my daughter's high school graduation—one of the great moments in life that celebrates achievement, this was a milestone. And what happened? My mind flooded with all the things we *didn't* do: The activities we never did together, and the trips we never took. I believe that many people are sitting at home, comparing themselves to others, and feeling the disconnection growing. I believe even more people are on the edge of disconnecting from society and are vulnerable to loneliness and isolation. This is an issue we can do something about, but we must recognize the need.

Numb from Loneliness: Sarah's Story

As I think about loneliness, I think of a conversation I had with Sarah, who told me about her relationship with her husband who struggled with an addiction to pornography and masturbation. His sex addiction had led to an intense need to masturbate multiple times a day. She told me about the countless nights she cries herself to sleep, feeling rejected and questioning her self-worth. She is married and desperately lonely. She craved physical intimacy with her husband, but she felt so distant from him that it was impossible. It was almost as if the pain from her personal life had numbed her to the world around her—even the kids running around her feet.

Every day she would put on a brave face, declare that everything was okay, and move along, but she carried a deep secret. She longed for a space where she could freely say, "I'm not okay. I'm sad, I'm hurt, and I'm lonely. I don't know what to do, and I don't know how to fix this." Her loneliness was closing in on her, and she felt trapped in this world where everything was supposed to be okay.

She said, "I feel like I'm living in the middle of this dark box, and the sides are closing in. It's much like what I imagine being in quicksand would be like. It's quickly sucking me under, where there will be no air, no life, and no space."

I can't even begin to imagine the pain that she was living in and the level of loneliness she was experiencing. To simply say that she has become numb is an understatement. As I've listened to these stories, and as the women talk to me about loneliness, I feel like there is a responsibility we all share to do something about it.

Speak Your Truth

We need to start speaking the truth, and we need to hear it. We need to know that we can say, "It's not okay right now. Today isn't a great day. Today is one of those days where I feel like I'm not making it and measuring up."

We need to create spaces whereby people can phone or text and let us know the depths of their loneliness. We need to get to the point where we're okay with the truth. Because when the truth of our loneliness is out, we can walk through anything. When we're able to say, "Hang on, here I am. I am lonely, and I feel alone, and I'm in the middle of all of these people, yet I feel like nobody sees me or hears me."

We need to be able to press the pause button on our own lives and be people who are willing to listen. I listened to people sob over their loneliness, and I felt a deep sense of understanding. I have not lived near my family now for over twenty years. I moved from Canada to Hong Kong when I was eighteen. Hong Kong is one of the busiest, fastest, and congested cities in the world, and I discovered that despite all of that, you could still feel very lonely.

Loneliness sometimes creeps onto the doorstep of my heart. In fact, just last week someone called and asked me, "How are you?"

I said, "I'm okay, but I'm having one of those weeks when I'm lonely." And it's not because of a lack of people around me, and it wasn't because I wasn't doing anything. I was very busy, and I had a lot of people around me, but I missed my mom. I was lonely for my mom. I was lonely for my sister. I was lonely, and the song from *Cheers* was dancing around in my head, "Sometimes you want to go where everybody knows your name, and they're always glad you came." I think of that *Cheers* song a lot. I've lived away from family and from those who have known me my entire life, and despite the great friends I have all over the world and where I live now, some days I just want to go where everybody knows my name, and they're always glad that I'm there.

I understand what loneliness feels like. It isn't a personality trait, and it isn't based on a people-type. It isn't based on age. It isn't selective. It happens to all of us, but for some, it can become serious enough to feel like they are stuck or trapped in it. We simply need to remember that people want to be seen and heard, and that requires us to make room for that to happen. We also need to remember that God is always with us and constantly available to us.

Friendship That Leads to Loneliness

Disappointments

Loneliness comes in many different forms, but one that deserves highlighting is where friendships are involved. Simply put, we get hurt in friendships. No matter how good of a friend someone is, and no matter how long we have been friends with them, no one is perfect. Our imperfections will eventually come out, and at some point, we will hurt others, and we will be hurt by others. It's going to happen.

What I've learned in my life is that it's important to prepare yourself for disappointment. That may sound a little negative and pessimistic, and I'm not suggesting we should expect the worst from people. What I *am* suggesting is that you learn to understand and accept that every relationship will eventually let you down—not because people are intrinsically bad, but because people are human and therefore flawed. When you prepare yourself for that reality, you can allow grace to flow more freely.

After all, we're just people, and we're all having a go at this thing called life. We're all making our way in the world today, and throughout our lives, we are bound to disappoint each other. As a friend, I'm going to disappoint. As a wife, I'm going to disappoint. As a parent, I'm going to disappoint. I'm not doing this intentionally; it's just a simple fact that our actions cannot live up to our expectations *all* of the time. If we enter into a relationship—be it platonic or romantic—with the understanding that both parties will experience disappointment at some point or another, and yet we choose to engage anyway, then perhaps we can minimize the sting of our inevitable offenses. That way, when it happens, it's not so hard to handle. It softens the blow, so to speak. And with that, forgiveness isn't far away. Forgiveness sits ready to be extended through grace, kindness, and respect.

handwritten margin notes: "stop expecting the world from people" "people are flawed just as I am" "it will"

A Practice from The Gathering Cloud

Retreating to Address Loneliness

1. This may seem paradoxical but find a block of time when you will be totally alone and uninterrupted for one to six hours. I highly recommend that you go outdoors or distinctly change the scenery from your everyday life. Nature is highly preferable, as it's often somewhere you may not come across any people. Avoid all technology-related distractions.

2. During this time, quiet your mind and choose to think on what is true, good, and beautiful.

Connecting to nature and using your senses may help you "smell the roses." The hyper-focus of your life may dissipate, as your attention moves to the experience of being connected to the world around you and the God who created it. Express your gratitude and sense God's presence with you. This exercise helps you learn to be alone without feeling lonely and is the path to true connectedness.

4

YOUR PAIN MATTERS
AND IS PART OF YOUR HEALING

*I have lived pain, and my life can tell; I only
deepen the wound of the world when I neglect
to give thanks for the heavy perfume of wild roses
in early July and the song of crickets on summer
humid nights and the rivers that run and the stars
that rise and the rain that falls and all the good
things that a good God gives.*

—ANN VOSKAMP[7]

Is a life without pain actually living? Take breathing, for example; as we breathe, we inhale and exhale. We can't do one without also doing the other; they work hand in hand to keep our hearts beating. Sleeping and waking are also things we need to experience in partnership. This is true of joy and sadness too. Without experiencing sadness, we wouldn't know joy. Without joy, we wouldn't know sadness. The Bible talks about how there is a time for everything:

> There's an opportune time to do things,
> a right time for everything on the earth:
> A right time for birth and another for death,
> A right time to plant and another to reap,
> A right time to kill and another to heal,
> A right time to destroy and another to construct,
> A right time to cry and another to laugh,
> A right time to lament and another to cheer,
> A right time to make love and another to abstain,
> A right time to embrace and another to part,
> A right time to search and another to count your losses,
> A right time to embrace and another to part,
> A right time to rip out and another to mend,
> A right time to shut up and another to speak up,
> A right time to love and another to hate,
> A right time to wage war and another to make peace.
> (Ecclesiastes 3:1–8, MSG)

I love that Scripture. It serves as a beautiful reminder that everything in life has a flow. If we rest in the push and pull of all things, and if we are patient enough to hear it, we can find harmony.

Have you ever noticed when little children fall on the playground, their mother or father will run to their side, pick them up, dust them off, and say, "Off you go. You're okay. All better." Often, this is all children need, but I wonder if it lays a bad foundation for how we deal with pain—especially emotional pain. This pick-up-and-carry-on mentality can bleed into places it shouldn't be, and then we find ourselves spouting off words that utterly lack compassion to people who are in pain: "You have to get over it and move on. There are plenty of fish in the sea," or "God obviously needed your baby in heaven." It's horrible! If we took time to consider some of these things that are often said to people who are hurting, I think we would be horrified by how we try to minimize and dust the pain away and move on.

Is this dusting away—this refusal to acknowledge pain more helpful or harmful? Are people walking around carrying a weight of pain that's pushing them down? What if we took time to acknowledge pain—be it a fall off the bike or the broken heart? Think of the times when someone has come alongside you and not offered answers or the magic pill to take it away, but instead just sat in the pain with you. Did that help you more than all the others who tried to offer you oversimplistic answers and quick fixes?

I think of the night my father died. Philip was away, the kids were in bed, and I received the call that my father, who had just been given a clean bill of health after his second round of multiple bypasses, had fallen to his knees fifty meters from my mother and father's front door. According to the friend who was with him, my father looked at him and said, "I'm in trouble."

Having had heart attacks before, I think my beautiful dad knew heaven was knocking, and he was being called forward. Upon hearing the news and trying to get in touch with Philip, who was at a concert in another city, I called my friend Tanya. Tanya lived over an hour away, but without hesitation she jumped in her car, drove to my home, and sat by my side. She had nothing to offer but her friendship and presence, and that was all I needed. She sat in my pain with me. She couldn't change the circumstances, and she couldn't make the loss any easier, but she could be with me. It was powerful. It was a gift, and it was a moment in time that I will never forget. Her presence was healing to me during a very hard night.

Listen to Your Heart: Lydia's Story

Lydia was a beautiful woman in her fifties whose life hadn't gone as she had hoped. Her husband had left her for a younger version of herself. Her kids were grown and living their own lives, and she was alone. Days turned into weeks, then months, and then years, and she found herself first realizing the pain she was living in as I listened to her on the other end of a Skype conversation.

Her solace was work and the people she engaged with throughout the week. They gave her purpose; they gave her strength. As I listened to her speak, I was reminded of how important we are to one another. It's true: If you want to see God, look into the eyes of the person sitting next to you. This woman's hope was found in the eyes and hearts of those who were alongside her every day. They didn't know their impact on her, but their words, their actions, their invitations to lunch and their kids' dance recitals were her lifeline.

Plato is credited with saying, "Be kind, for everyone you meet is fighting a hard battle." Have you ever stopped to think about the opportunities for kindness that are presented to us every day? The smile exchanged at the supermarket checkout, or the polite "thank you" when ordering a coffee, or the chance to tell a loved one how beautiful they are; these can be invaluable to the people with whom we interact.

Do you ever feel that internal prompting to text someone, to show up at their house with flowers, or simply to call someone for some good conversation? Maybe that's God speaking to you. Maybe he's highlighting the significance you could have in someone else's life. Can I suggest that the next time you feel that prompting, you respond and allow yourself to be fully present in that moment. Allow yourself the blessing to be who you are meant to be: One who responds to the inner calling. Allow yourself room to understand that prompting and to hear that small voice. These are opportunities for us to allow our true selves to respond to the human need that is directly in front of us: to dance with the divine.

Scientists are working hard to research into the idea that the heart has its own brain of sorts that often processes information before our brain does. This could offer insight into some of the feelings we have, such as empathy. Studies at the HeartMath Research Center have detected that the electromagnetism of an individual's heart can affect and even synchronize with another individual's brain waves when standing up to five feet apart from one another. In short, the brain seems to be innately sensitive and receptive to the heart "energy" of others.[8]

Whenever our hearts prompt us to reach out to someone, these are opportunities to connect with people whose private lives are painful or perhaps in shambles—people like Lydia. We can brighten the lives of the people around us simply by showing kindness.

The Walking Dead

Pain is a part of life—oftentimes a big part. This is what I've learned from my forty plus years on earth. Between the countless conversations I had while gathering the research for this book to the interactions I have with people on a daily basis, I have come to understand that people are in pain, and in many cases, people are suffering under the pressure of living with it.

I once listened to a pastor speak about how he had been a paramedic before becoming a pastor. He told a story about how paramedics watch for what they refer to as "the walking dead" whenever they tend to people involved in severe accidents. The walking dead are the individuals involved in an accident who appear to be less hurt than the others, but in reality they may have sustained far worse injuries—perhaps even be fatal—if left untreated. Typically, the paramedic-turned-pastor said, the walking dead are the ones who are able to offer the most information about the accident.

I think of this idea of the walking dead a lot, especially when it comes to the women I interviewed. So many seemed to fit that category of the walking dead. They were still standing, moving about, and interacting on the outside, but they had died on the inside. They had become numb.

Put on Your Big-Girl Undies

Pain is okay. It has a way of making us dig deeply within ourselves. Sure, it's never enjoyable, but what if we embraced it anyway? And I don't mean in a masochistic sense, but imagine if we simply acknowledge when someone hurts us. What if we welcome pain and recognize it for what it is rather than sweep it under the carpet?

For years I have espoused the saying, "Put on your big-girl undies." I still like that saying, but what it used to mean to me was, "Seriously, just get over it and get on with it." I've come to realize that this is a prescription rather than a reflection, and reflection is such a necessary part of walking through pain. Sadly, in the past I probably would have told Lydia to put on her big-girl undies and get over it. I now realize that prescription doesn't help Lydia process anything. It's a bandage approach with a motivational twist. Instead, the best thing I can do is empathize with Lydia and simply be present with her.

When my father died, one of my closest friends, Michaela, said something so wise to me. She said, "Grief is messy, uncomfortable, and sometimes ugly, but the only way to healing is through it, so you need to keep walking." She was so right, and although it was tough to hear at the time, I needed those words. I needed to know that I had to walk through the valley of grief, which requires two steps. First, I had to engage my need to grieve without denying the pain I felt. Second, I didn't need to set up camp and live there; I needed to keep walking.

Now, nine years after his sudden death, feelings of grief still suddenly spark and wash over me sometimes, so much so that the loss feels like it was just yesterday. Now, instead of ignoring it and sweeping it away, I choose to acknowledge the grief. I welcome it in one breath, and in the next breath I let it go and welcome God into that space. I enter a flow of healing that doesn't ignore the pain or attempt to motivate me out of it; rather, I give myself permission to grieve, to process, and to open my heart once again for God to fill me with healing love. Then I can put my big-girl undies on and move forward.

It's true that the big-girl undies are still a necessary part of the healing equation. However, if we put them on *after* grieving, they fit a heck of a lot better. Then we are ready to move forward with confidence, hope, and peace in our hearts.

Embracing Pain

I first learned the importance of grieving through pain during the early years of my marriage when Philip and I started trying to have children. I always dreamed of being a mother, and the thought of raising kids excited me. Being in an interracial marriage, I would get lost wondering what our children would look like and wonder how the beautiful blending of our genes would work in our offspring.

We had been married for four years, and we had been as selfish as we wanted to be. We both felt it was time to start trying to conceive. What we weren't prepared for was the endometriosis diagnosis from my doctor during a routine visit to my doctor. I had it, and it was bad. In fact, my gynecologist told me it was so bad that my chances of ever becoming pregnant were slim.

I was heartbroken, but I wasn't lacking hope. Sitting across from the doctor, I accepted the sobering news, gave myself a moment to process, then I looked him in the eye and said, "I will have a baby. There is a promise of that, and I'm holding onto it." With that, I left the office, and my pursuit to become pregnant started. Surprisingly, it didn't take long before I was holding a stick with a plus sign on it. We could hardly contain ourselves!

We proceeded with all the normal precautionary wisdom. My doctor confirmed the pregnancy and told me that there was no medical reason why I should be pregnant, but he agreed with me that miracles do happen. We made it through the early stages of pregnancy and passed all the early markers, which allowed us to begin sharing our good news. It all felt right. Against all odds, we were starting our little family.

All was as it should be until one frightful day when I was working from home and started to bleed. Parts of that day are now a little blurry. I can't remember where Philip was, and I don't remember why, but for whatever reason, he didn't come with me to the doctor. The bleeding was intense, and I knew in an instant that something was wrong. I arrived at my doctor's office, he examined me, and I had miscarried.

I remember getting cleaned up and watching my miscarried fetus be discarded into a rubbish bin—unattended and gone. I sat across from my doctor in his office as he delivered the news that crushed my young heart. He told me that although un-expected by him, I could get pregnant, but the endometriosis would prevent me from carrying a baby to term.

I sat cold, alone, and aching on my way home in a taxicab, but my heart and mind were still in that room, standing by the rubbish bin, looking at the life that was lost, and feeling empti-ness in my womb. I wasn't given time to say goodbye, not that I had any idea how to even do that. I had no maturity to carry me through those minutes, days, and weeks ahead. Was my doc-tor correct? Would I never have children? Was my dream being crushed? Was I crushing Philip's dream too? How do I tell people I failed—that my body couldn't do what a woman's body is designed for? Was I alone in this?

Not a day goes by that I don't think of that first baby. Miscarriage is a crazy thing. I understand why and how it happens, but no one prepares you for it. It happens in silence, and it's not a popular story of loss, yet so many of us walk around forever carrying the heartache of that silent loss.

It was my mother who really helped me through this time. She gave me the maturity and courage to walk through the grief I was experiencing. She told me to mourn the loss of that child and not just get on with life. She encouraged me to embrace the emotions I was feeling and to give myself time to grieve. She is such a wise woman, and I'm grateful for her wisdom throughout my life.

After the necessary healing time, I was given the cautionary green light to try again. My doctor advised me of expected outcomes while Philip and I prayed and believed for the promise of a child to be fulfilled. Twelve months later, we welcomed our beautiful Sophia into the world, and life took an entirely new direction.

Your Pain Can Lead to Healing

I'd like to tell you that it took a matter of weeks before I found my mojo again, but I can't. I can tell you that I felt pain. I breathed it, I held it, and I did exactly what I needed to do: I embraced and felt that pain and moved forward. Fast forward to today and ask me how I am. I still remember the awful event at the doctor's office like it was yesterday. I still feel the loss, but that's just it. I feel it, I acknowledge it, and I move on. I've heard it said before, "If you can feel it, you can heal it." We need to allow ourselves to feel so we can heal.

I often say, "Breathe in God, breathe out tension or pain." I never really understood how profound this was. I used to throw this phrase around as a joke or a comment to bring a bit of levity into situations. Over the years, however, I've realized this throwaway comment rings true. When we recognize our pain, our healing is in front of us. When we name it, embrace it, and acknowledge it, we can move through it.

In the labor and delivery room we are told to channel our pain into energy for giving birth, and I think this same advice is true of other experiences too. When we quiet our hearts, minds, and spirits, we can flow into the healing process. The space without words is so loud and tells us that in the quiet there is healing. In the quiet there is health, and in the quiet, we not only heal but we also learn.

Our pain can lead to healing. Having lost my father so suddenly and allowing myself the time to walk through it has brought me to a place of spiritual maturity that I never knew was possible. Through the pain of divorce, betrayal, or abuse, there is space for healing. By quieting our minds and souls, we allow that still small voice to whisper to us, saying, "You know this space, you've been here, and we will move through this." Whether you have been like me, lying on the bathroom floor and cradling my head in my arms, or you're out with friends and have your brave face on, pain is there. It's real, and it's ours to walk through.

A Practice from The Gathering Cloud

Retreating to Deal with Pain

1. Find a quiet place and calm your thoughts and emotions.

2. Take note of any physical pain you feel. Place your hand on the part of your body that hurts. Acknowledge the pain and invite God to bring comfort and healing to the pain by saying, "I welcome your presence, God. Comfort and heal me."

3. Take note of any mental or emotional pain you feel. Place your hand on your head for mental pain and on your heart for emotional pain. Acknowledge the pain and invite God to bring comfort and healing to the pain by saying, "I welcome your presence, God. Comfort and heal me."

4. This exercise gives us the opportunity to feel, which is to be fully human, while inviting God into this experience, which is fully divine. Answers often come through stillness. Express gratitude for God's peace, love, and healing presence.

5

ADDICTED

We suffer to get well. We surrender to win.
We die to live. We give it away to keep it.

—Richard Rohr, *Breathing Under Water*[9]

Have you binged eight hours of Netflix lately? Did you check
your phone 150 times today? Millennials do.[10] As Richard Rohr
says in his groundbreaking book *Breathing Under Water*, "We are
all addicts." We live in the most addictive and addicted global
society in history. The world economy thrives on it as people
become addicted to consumerism, growth, debt, social media,
technology, self-projection, and our own thinking, let alone the
big three: alcohol, drugs, and porn.

I want to focus on the addiction to porn because of the
storm it has caused in our social consciousness. It's almost uni-
versally accessible at no cost, and it encourages objectification,
particularly of women. It has wreaked havoc at every level of the
human experience—the brain, relationships, and society. Porn

negatively affects women of all ages and is a destructive force in intimate relationships.

Porn Addiction

Porn addiction has been considered shameful for as long as it's been around. People hide their addictions to it, but so many people are struggling that the conversation is hard to avoid. As porn has become normalized as a part of society—just like teenage drinking or marijuana use, it's no longer a taboo subject.

The online porn industry itself is firmly part of popular culture. Netflix has its *Hot Girls Wanted* documentary, which follows the lives of young girls entering the industry. Public figures such as Tiger Woods and Charlie Sheen engage in relationships with porn stars. And, of course, habitually watching online porn is often a gateway to webcam sex, technology-assisted prostitution, or risky sex with strangers. It is a telling sign of our times that this whole industry is referred to as the "adult" industry. But telling people you are a sex or porn addict, or that you live with one is still a rare thing.

One recurring narrative I've heard from women who are addicted to porn, or women whose partners are sex addicts, or women who have found the visual standards and sexual acts depicted in porn completely unrealistic is they unanimously agree that porn has not only been a factor in their feeling inadequate, alienated, hurt, and ashamed of their sexual identity and self-image, but it has also affected their sexual encounters.

As women, we're in a fight for equality, but the porn industry is becoming increasingly degrading. Such is the bizarre dance we are in, and it just doesn't make sense. When the truth is out, you can walk through anything, but men and women have suffered in silence for a long time because of porn. We need to break the silence and say, "We hear you, this has nothing to do with you, and you're not alone."

Sex Is Everywhere

Turn on the television at 7:30 p.m. Look at Instagram posts from teenage girls. Walk through your local shopping center. Check out a billboard. We are bombarded with images that scream sex.

I recall walking through the shopping center a few years ago with my son who was twelve at the time. He was looking at all the advertising and made a comment that has stuck with me. He felt overwhelmed by the number of scantily clad women in the images pasted all throughout the center. He said he wasn't sure where to look. At twelve years old, he didn't know if he should look into the eyes of these women or finish undressing them in his mind.

I could see the mixed message racing through his brain. As a boy, he was told to value girls, respect them, and treat them with honor. He has two sisters who he loves and adores, yet everything around him was telling him just the opposite. Was it the clothes, perfume, or travel advertisements? Or was it the dream of what this girl was offering—the lure of sex? Everywhere we look, we see message after message encouraging us to look, touch, and taste.

This is no joking matter. According to a study conducted at the University of Nebraska, the average age when males are first exposed to pornography is 13.37 years old.[11] What was concerning about this study was that the younger the age of first exposure, the more likely these boys were to develop a desire to have power over a woman. The older a man was at first exposure, it was more likely they would engage in "playboy" behavior. It appears that the older a man is when introduced to pornography, the more it has to do with promiscuity, but the younger they are, the more it has to do with the power dynamic.

When young teenage boys access pornography, it has a real impact on their attitudes toward gender roles, which is so prevalent in the type of behavior now brought to light in the #MeToo movement. I have listened to several women cry over not knowing how to teach their sons the value of women and the gravity of sex because their husbands encourage it. Pornography is a major problem—within homes, marriages, partnerships, and in raising kids.

Is Porn Enslaving Us?

What is happening to us? And, before I start, may I just say that this isn't only a male challenge. Women are increasingly struggling with porn addiction, and the number of women I spoke to during the interviews who said they were addicted to porn was alarming. It is a struggle. They crave it, and then they beat themselves up for engaging in it. They feel deep shame, regret, and anger, and more often than not the anger works itself out on those they love most.

This is the cycle of addiction. The trouble is, while we won't crave other drugs until we've tried them, puberty biologically awakens sexual desire. From there, porn is so readily available and accessible that many well-meaning young people turn to it as an outlet only to become entangled in addiction. That's where the cycle starts, but like any other addiction, the accompanying feeling of shame is a key part of the cycle's power. It keeps its users silent. Why don't we talk about it openly? Why is it that we stay silent until it's often too late?

Martin Daubney was the longest-serving editor of the men's magazine *Loaded*. At the time of its launch in 1994, *Loaded* was deemed to be a new magazine dedicated to life, liberty, and the pursuit of sex, drinks, football, and other less serious matters. Daubney had his "come-to-Jesus" moment when his son was four years old, and Daubney somehow stumbled on research that says young boys' first experience with porn will be at ten, and then their use of pornography can snowball if left to their own devices. Daubney now spends much of his time tweeting and sharing anti-porn messages such as, "Porn was meant to empower us. But is it enslaving us? And if it is, why aren't more men angry about it?"[12]

If you question whether porn is addictive, all you have to do is talk to someone who is battling it. Whether it be a man or a woman, their stories are largely the same. They can't get through the day without it. I recently talked to someone who is a recovering sex addict. He told me he had to retrain his brain because it was so wired to porn that he needed his daily—if not hourly—fix, and it wasn't just viewing it that satisfied him; he needed progressively more intense "hits," just like a drug addict. It affects every part of an addict's life: their relationships with others, their relationship with themselves, their self-care, their thoughts, and the list goes on.

FightTheNewDrug.org, a nonprofit and online porn addiction awareness website, explains that porn addiction affects us in three main ways: our brains, our relationships, and our society. According to a University of Cambridge study published in the journal *PLOS One*, "Pornography triggers brain activity in people with compulsive sexual behavior, known commonly as sex addiction, similar to that triggered by drugs in the brains of drug addicts."[13]

Peer-reviewed research featured on FightTheNewDrug.org cites studies that have found that "frequency of porn use correlates with depression, anxiety, stress, and social problems, with clear differences in the brain activity of people with compulsive sexual behavior and those without."[14] Porn stimulates the brain's reward center, affecting brain chemistry and neural pathways.

Beyond the effects on the brain, studies have found that "porn use has been found to influence some users' sexual preferences, leaving them wanting what they've seen on screen and significantly less satisfied with sex in real life."[15] Furthermore, "After being exposed to pornography, men reported being less satisfied with their partner's physical appearance and level of affection, and express greater desire for sex without emotional involvement."[16]

What does this mean for society? "Among the effects of the use of pornography are an increased negative attitude towards women, decreased empathy for victims of sexual violence, and an increase in dominating and sexually imposing behavior."[17] The US Department of Justice and the National Center for Missing and Exploited Children both recognize that pornography is an element that adds to the serious problem of sex trafficking.

The side effects of porn last longer than the side effects listed for a medication in a commercial, so why do people still think porn is harmless? We need to have these conversations—both making room for addicts to safely confess their struggles without shame and warning the next generation of porn's dangers, so they run from it like the drug it is.

A Tragic First Encounter: John's Story

John was trapped from his first encounter with porn at the tender age of thirteen when he was at a friend's birthday party, and his friend's mom threw all her husband's magazines and hardcore videos on the bed and said, "Here you go, boys. We are off to bed. Have fun." He had never seen anything like it. His viewing habits increased after that, and he wanted more. He dove into the world that changed him and plagued him for thirty-five years. Now at forty-nine and clean for a year, he said it took a rewiring of his brain to set him free.

Locked in this world of shame, secrets, and acting out, he stumbled through life lying, covering up, and spending money to feed his addiction. He was lost, broken, and trapped in a world of darkness that knew no light. His life was filled with lashing out at those who loved him and spending time in lonely, dark rooms on webcams and in dimly lit clubs.

It all started with porn thrown onto a bed at a birthday party sleepover. Did all the boys from that night become sex addicts from one seemingly innocent offering by a mother who chose a strange way to celebrate her son's "coming of age?" No, not all of them. Some left it there that night and never picked it up again, but for this one man it was like heroin, and today, at forty-nine years old, he admits he is a recovering addict and has committed himself to a life of sobriety and spirituality. I can only hope John's story of recovery will become less rare. All too often, including most of the addicts I have spoken with, these men and women are still struggling, leaving behind devastated marriages, relationships, and lives.

Wedding Night Anxiety: Jill's Story

This problem, as I said earlier, isn't unique to men. During the interviews, I spoke to a beautiful young woman who was weeks away from standing at the altar with the man of her dreams, ready to commit her life to walk with him. Jill too was plagued by the images burned into her mind from porn. Would she enjoy her wedding night, or would she secretly jump onto her computer once he was asleep and escape into her secret world?

Her future husband knew of her struggle, and he too struggled in this area. They suffered in silence, wanting desperately to be rid of this thing that held them captive and separate from one another. She described feelings of entrapment—unable to fully engage and live in the present the way she wanted. Shame shrouded what could be. Would she ever feel free and able to live fully, especially in her new marriage?

Codependency

I think it's important to pause here and take a moment to address each one of you who may be walking with someone through their painful valley of sex addiction. It may be your partner, your child, or a friend; whatever the case may be, it's important to remind yourself that the addiction has nothing to do with you. If you are the partner of someone who is struggling, it's easy to go down the path of questioning everything about yourself. Your self-esteem can take a beating, and you must do whatever you can to remind yourself it isn't about you. It has never been and never will be about you.

As for the glossy, airbrushed images that you associate with porn, know that they are just that: glossy, airbrushed images. They aren't real. Do yourself a favor and watch *Body Evolution: Model Before and After* on YouTube, or Google images of pornstars without their makeup. It will help put things into perspective. Ultimately, understand that while all comparison is damaging, this area of comparison is entirely unfair. No matter who you are, you wouldn't be able to compete with an entire team of professional makeup artists, computer graphic designers, and a film crew that costs millions of dollars to only show the "best" of unrealistic and irreplicable images.

While your partner became an addict on their own, I would be remiss not to say that as the addict's partner, it is very common to become what is known as the addict's caretaker, or someone who enables codependency. According to Mental Health America, "The caretaker often acts in an expression of love, sacrificing their own needs for the needs of the addict, covering for or controlling their behavior, or managing aspects of their life because they are no longer able, and this may become compulsive for 'the helper.'"[18] This relationship between addiction and codependency is well documented and was first evident in studies of families of alcoholics in the 1950s.

If you are reading this and feel the tug inside you saying that you have been enabling your partner in their addiction, please know there is help available to both of you. This is a fight worth fighting because your relationship is worth fighting for. I strongly encourage you to be courageous and consider therapy for yourself and your relationship.

You're Already on Your Way

If you break your silence, seek therapy for you and your partner, and stick with it, you will recover. How do I know this? Because you're reading this. Maybe you bought the book, or maybe someone gave it to you as a gift, or maybe someone has told you to just read this chapter because someone is finally talking about pornography addiction. Whatever the case may be, I know you'll make it because you are here.

You may be filled with anger, frustration, or tears because something you've read here has resonated with you. I'm so proud of you regardless of how you got here; you're here. I'm seriously fist-pumping the air right now, doing the happy dance, and if I could, I would be wrapping my arms around you and giving you the biggest hug you have ever experienced.

You need to know that you will make it because you love deeply, and you feel. That alone is huge. You haven't turned off your emotional dial. You haven't given up and adopted an attitude that only leads to bitterness and ugliness. You are pursuing love and wholeness, and you know it's there; it's out there somewhere for the taking.

You aren't alone. So many people have sat and are sitting where you are today. Yes, they feel defeated, unloved, unattractive, unwanted, and so many more un's that I could add as well. But what's the point of the un's? They are *all* lies. You aren't defeated, you aren't unloved, you aren't unattractive, and you aren't unwanted; you are strong, loved, attractive, wanted, and so much more. I believe in you, and my hope is that you hear "Eye of the Tiger," the theme song from *Rocky*, playing in your head as you read this.

You're already on your way. Yes, you have some hard yards

ahead of you. You're going to have to make tough decisions and have tough conversations, but that's so much of life. Join me in taking the lid off this conversation, and let's walk this out together—no more shame, no more guilt, and no more sadness. We're in this together, and we are going to cheer one another on, reminding each other that we will make it because we are seen, and we are heard.

Recovery: The Twelve Steps and Spirituality

As with many addictions, the path to recovery is typically long, mainly because most people have been addicts for a long time before they are able to admit their powerlessness over their addiction. Their use often stems from another source of pain and has been ingrained into their perspective on life. The physiological and neurological paths of habit have become so hard-wired into their brains that it cannot be unwound in an instant. Willpower or "white-knuckling" through their temptation is ultimately a futile effort. Although it may thwart many episodes of "acting out," it does not stamp out the source of their addiction.

I want to mention *Breathing Under Water* again, in which Rohr merges contemplative spirituality and the Twelve Steps of Alcoholics Anonymous, which is still the foundation to most recovery programs for all sorts of addictions. He observed that while spirituality—particularly Christian spirituality—focused on thoughts and beliefs about salvation and enlightenment, and "pushed this great liberation off into the next world, Twelve Steppers settled for mere sobriety from a substance instead of a real transformation of the self."

Rohr posits four assumptions about addictions: "We are all addicts; that 'stinking thinking' (holding on to how we do anything, especially our pattern of thought) is the universal addiction; that all societies are addicted to themselves and creates deep codependency on them; and that some form of alternative consciousness is the only freedom from this self and from cultural lies." What brings change? What does Rohr say is the key to recovery? "We must surrender our ego to the love and trust of God and commune with God through prayer where we break down all the lies we believe as true in our false self and start living out of our true self—deeply connected and grounded in spirituality."[19]

Remember John who struggled with porn for decades? I have seen surrender and prayer at the heart of his transformation. I have seen the grip of addiction dissipate as he has started to live out of his true self.

Resources for Recovery

Whether you are the porn or sex addict, or whether you have one in your world, you need to get educated about it. FightTheNewDrug.org is a great place to start. It details how porn addiction affects the brain, relationships, and society. Fight the New Drug is particularly focused on youth and millennials and aims to bring awareness through high schools and universities. It offers online resources for recovery and for parents to address pornography with their children.

There are also recovery programs you can easily find for all forms of addictions: alcohol, drugs, overeating, sex, and porn. For porn, sex, and relationship addictions, you can look for these organizations:

Sexaholics Anonymous

Sex Addicts Anonymous

Sex and Love Addicts Anonymous

Many of these groups meet in church buildings, and there are online meetings for those who don't live in cities that offer in-person meetings. I cannot speak to the efficacy of these programs personally, but what I can say is that it is freeing to be in a room with people who are struggling with the same issues as you and who speak openly and vulnerably without fear of judgment. In our society of competition and comparison, this is a rare thing.

The key to recovery groups is that you are not alone. Everyone is in it together. The dismantling of the isolation and secrecy is powerful, and by shining light on the matter, we can start to see clearly. Addicts have told me that recovery groups can feel depressing, as you see members who have been sober for thirty years come in for the next meeting to disclose that they relapsed. Understand that simply attending the meetings will not fix your addiction. You need to do the work; you need to work the steps.

Take one day at a time to make life a little less overwhelming. Spirituality is central to the Twelve Steps. In fact, step two says, "Come to believe that a power greater than ourselves could restore us to sanity." This can mean that, like John, you develop a contemplative spiritual practice. Read *Breathing Under Water*. Better yet, do it with another addict. Join a recovery group. Get a sponsor. Do the steps. Surrender your ego. Have a relationship of love and trust with God. I do sincerely pray that you or the addict in your life will find peace and freedom in the journey of recovery.

I end this chapter with the Serenity Prayer, which is read and spoken at many recovery groups around the world:

> God, grant me the serenity to accept
> the things I cannot change,
> courage to change the things I can,
> and wisdom to know the difference.[20]

A Practice from The Gathering Cloud

Retreating to Deal with Addiction

Daily surrender of ego and trust in a loving God brings a gentle transformation within the core of ourselves and removes us from our addictions and attachments. The following practice is taken from the fifteenth century prayer of St. Nicholas of Flue:[21]

1. Find a quiet place away from distraction. (Turn off your phone!)

2. Bring to mind all that keeps you separated from the love of God (your addictions, shame, fear, anxiety, worry, etc.) and symbolically open your hands on your lap and "place" these things in them.

3. Say, "God, take everything from me that keeps me from you." As you say this, raise your hands upward slightly, as if you are offering them to God in surrender.

4. With your hands still raised in front of you, bring to mind all that would bring you closer to God (love, trust, peace, faith, hope, etc.) and say, "God, give everything to me that brings me near to you."

5. Continuing with your palms up, raise your hands above your head, as if to offer up to God your very self and say, "God, take me away from myself and give me completely to you."

6. Express gratitude to God.

6

YOUR INTRINSIC VALUE

*One of the greatest regrets in life
is being what others would want you to be,
rather than being yourself.*

—SHANNON L. ALDER

Connectedness is the true masterpiece of relationships, and when lived well it's a stunning view. But all too often we get in our own way and prevent true connectedness from ever happening. I get to spend a lot of time with people, and one of the things I have seen is that we look to others to discern our own value.

Take a husband and a wife, for example. Until they get married, they have for the most part traveled through life as individuals who managed themselves. What seems to happen, however, is that for whatever reason, once we've heard the words, "You may kiss the bride," we begin to derive worth and value from what our spouse thinks of us, feels toward us, and how they speak to us. Men sometimes do this, but in my experience, it's predominantly a thing we do as women, and since I'm speaking to women, that's where I'll focus.

"You Complete Me"

"You complete me," is the famous line from the film *Jerry McGuire*. The title character played by Tom Cruise has fallen from grace in his professional life, but he realizes he's fallen in love with a single mom named Dorothy. He awkwardly arrives to profess his love and stumbles into a scene of Dorothy's older sister hosting her divorcée small group. Jerry tells Dorothy, "I love you. You … complete me."

Dorothy replies, "Shut up. Just shut up. You had me at hello."

I understand this line in a new way now. Over the course of the last few years, I've been in a mentoring situation with an exceptional older woman in my life named Susanna. I am the mentee, and this woman is wise. Not only is she wise, but we also occasionally go on walks together. At sixty-six years old, she schools me in fitness. I have a lot to learn from her mentally, spiritually, and physically. She once asked me a question that challenged me: "Do you need your husband, and do you need your kids?"

My response to her was that I didn't need my husband (we were in such a rough place at the time she asked me this that I wasn't sure I even wanted him), but I needed my kids. She replied, "Okay, we'll turn that around."

I didn't quite understand what was about to transpire over the next few months with her, but I'm forever grateful for the journey she took me on. She explained to me how I needed to get to a place where I didn't need anyone or anything except God. She said that in and through my relationship with Him, I would find my way back to myself, which would lead me to wholeness.

I struggled with this notion, especially when it came to my kids. I needed my kids. They were my life, and although I didn't find my worth or value in them, I needed them. They were like air to my lungs, and I felt like I was disrespecting them or leaving them unprotected by even whispering the words, "I don't need my kids."

As I leaned into the idea and met weekly with Susanna, she led me further and further into the heart of God, and I found myself in God and God in me. It was through listening and practicing the presence of God, spending time intentionally until, breath by breath, my heart began to beat in sync with something beyond me. I entered a holy flow that fed my soul, heart, and mind, and there was a connection of the three. I experienced true connectedness by coming back to myself through God, and it was in that space that I was able to say I no longer needed my kids or Philip, but I desperately wanted them. I wanted to be connected to them in a way that allowed me to be fully myself in my relationship with them, and I wanted them to be fully themselves—free to love with unbridled passion.

This truly was the beginning of something so freeing in my life. Was Jerry McGuire really not a complete person without Dorothy? Did he derive all his emotional needs and self-esteem from her? Isn't "you complete me" a textbook example of co-dependence? It would appear so, which I still think is really a bummer. Could something so romantic be harmful?

It isn't your husband's responsibility to give you your sense of worth or value. They aren't designed to do that. Imagine that pressure. I can confidently say anyone will be disappointed if they're looking for their personal worth and value in and through their partner. It's just not going to be enough nor should it. It's not the job or role of a significant other to fill.

Your worth and value come from God, and it is up to you to take that journey and find out what that means for you. When it comes from God, then it won't matter what your life or relationship throws at you because you're not reliant upon it for anything other than freely giving and receiving the love that is given back to you. Seriously, take the pressure off each other and allow your connectedness to flow from your heart, which is connected to the Creator of the universe who speaks life into you, over you, and through you.

Speak to yourself and let your inner narrative be one of lovingkindness. From that place you can extend yourself in a loving and kind way. We must firstly be connected to God. Then we extend into the world and connect with hearts and minds in a way that is life-giving and life-affirming.

In the same way, we can't look for our worth or value from our relationships with our kids. They have enough pressure on them as it is, and the last thing they need is to feel like they are responsible for filling your value tank. And if you put that pressure on them, be prepared to be disappointed and hurt. They weren't designed to fill that for you any more than your husband, and you will be let down. Your connection to your children is so much richer when you approach parenting from a place of wholeheartedness because that's where true connectivity is formed.

Simply put, do the work. Put in the hard yards, go deep internally with God, so you can go wide and long with your love and connectivity to your partner and children. And lastly, take the pressure off yourself. You aren't designed to give that to anyone either. But what you can do and how you can impact the lives of your children and your husband is to go on this journey yourself. Find your value in and through God and then be. Be who you are meant to be and let them see the transformation in your life. Through this you will unknowingly lead them to their source: God.

Decide What You Want to Change

So far and for most of these pages, I've encouraged you to acknowledge the pain you've lived or continue to live in, but now I'm talking about building connectivity with perhaps the very people who hurt you. This may seem like a bit of a switch. How does this make sense?

As I've said, acknowledging our pain is a necessary step, but it isn't the final one. We don't pitch a tent in our pain and stay there. The goal is to find truth in our pain that helps us release it, so that we can engage more fully in life again. A significant part of that engagement is connectivity to family. Just like branches on a tree, when we lose connection, we actually lose life.

In pursuing connection, we're going to have to decide what we want to change. We all face a time where we realize we are fed up with whatever it is we are dealing with. It could be constantly nagging your kids to pick things up, a situation at work, or something with your partner that you have dealt with for years. Maybe it's your weight or an anger issue. I'm not sure what it is that you deal with, but we all have areas that need attention, growth, and development. I think it's imperative that we take time to take a good hard look at ourselves, identify our areas that need attention, and in and through self-realization begin the process of change.

All I can say is thank God for our therapist. My husband and I have decided that we will not carry on through life without therapy being part of the equation. I've heard it said before and most likely you have too, but we take our cars in for service more than we do our bodies. We neglect the condition of our hearts and stumble through life hoping for a better day without having changed our oil in years.

For us, the decision for therapy came after a long stream of arguments, frustration, anger, and constant irritation with one another. I had sunk to a place where even the way Philip chewed irritated me. Hormones or not, I would turn into what I can only describe as Shrek with PMS. I found myself sinking into a pit of anger and each passing day it was building. It wasn't pretty, and I was so over it. I knew I had to do something, and it had to start with me. I decided to go on my own journey of discovery rather than seething my way through life.

The Power of a Praying Wife

I spent time with Susanna, my mentor, and she asked me if I wanted to walk through a book called *The Power of a Praying Wife*. I was honest with her and told her that in my state, I wasn't confident that she would want to hear my prayers. Being the incredible woman she is, she wasn't fazed by a word I said and began to walk me through it, week in and week out. I experienced such a change; it was truly a lifeline thrown to me as I was drowning. I'm forever grateful to Susanna for embracing me in my pain and walking with me one step at a time.

Let's be honest. At the time, I wished it was about Philip, not me. But through this, I realized what needed to change was me. I tell my kids all the time, "The only person you can change is you," and there I was discovering I needed to change all along. I realized my takeaway lesson from *The Power of a Praying Wife* had more to do with the power and ability to change from within.

Throughout our time together I could see change. I would text Susanna with revelation about myself. We would laugh about how the ways I once thought so wise were in fact pride and ego in the way of my true self. I needed to let ego and pride step aside, so the true Susan could emerge and become part of my story.

We often look at change in a negative way. Change can be hard and frustrating when we do it in our own strength, but when we do it in God's strength, it is transformational from the inside out, and change becomes something we crave. It's like exercise. If we're honest, exercise isn't one of those jump-off-your-seats kind of things we long to do, but when we make it a habit, our bodies start to crave it. By day seven we are bursting with energy and excited to go for our walk, workout, swim, or whatever, but it takes effort and honesty to reach the day when the momentum starts to sustain us. Change is the same, and I can't wait to walk you through another contemplative moment at the end of this chapter, where we embrace the idea of change.

Walk It out One Decision at a Time

I never want to make change sound easy. I want to acknowledge it's often hard, especially if you are in a relationship where the other person isn't changing. The people around us can always add interesting or difficult dynamics to our process of change, but often, just like with being vulnerable, as people see us changing it gives them permission to change as well.

Change comes when we acknowledge what needs to be changed, and we quiet our hearts to simply breathe in life and allow our minds to relax into our hearts. It's the meeting of these where revelation and transformation take place with God.

That popular phrase of letting go and letting God is true when we truly surrender to a greater power. I'm so grateful I've come to a place where I accept that I'm not in control, and the Spirit of God will lead me: "I will always show you where to go. I'll give you a full life in the emptiest of places—firm muscles, strong bones. You'll be like a well-watered garden, a gurgling spring that never runs dry" (Isaiah 58:10–11 MSG). In the stillness and in the quiet, I discover my path—where to place my feet, when to speak, and when to be soft. I dream of being a well-watered garden that gives life to those around me.

As you embrace change, understand that it is a process. Change comes one decision at a time. Sometimes the decisions will be big ones, but more often than not it's the small, timely decisions that bring lasting change. Sometimes it's moment by moment, breath by breath, where we let go of our need to be right in the midst of a heated conversation. It's in those moments that we embrace what is happening on the inside. We are propelled to the next level of change one step at a time—one decision at a time. Then when we look in the rearview mirror of life, change has happened without us even noticing it. We will find that change has come in the quiet, in the constant, and in the deepest parts of our being. This is what builds confidence.

More than that, not only our life changes, but also the lives of those around us. That is how we become light and love.

Negotiables and Non-Negotiables

As I interviewed women for this book, and as I reflect on my own life, I have learned that a time comes when we have to draw a line in the sand. We have to determine what our negotiables and non-negotiables are. What will we stand for? What is our truth? What battles will we fight? What hills will we die on? What things aren't perfect, but we are willing to live with?

I remember speaking to one woman who shared her story about her ex-husband who constantly belittled her for years. She was a beautiful woman who began to erode from within over the years because of the constant belittling and control. She decided to take her power back. Surrounded by the love and support of her family and friends, one decision and brave step at a time, she began to find her voice and live stronger and more confident every day. She decided to draw a line in the sand and put her worth on the side of the sand that was a non-negotiable. She would no longer subject herself to his belittling or control.

She initially did this with little things; she would take a class while he was away on extended work trips. She began to take back herself and place value on herself by learning and experiencing life. She bravely, boldly, and systematically built her life back one small decision at a time. Today, she is building her own brand, inviting people into her world, and encouraging them to live stronger, healthier, happier lives. I have stood on the digital sidelines and cheered her on with every Facebook Live video she posts, every update she puts out, every moment of bravery she has walked. I have seen firsthand how choosing to extend forgiveness to someone who kept her under an unthinkable level of control and manipulation for years has brought freedom into her life.

She drew a line in the sand. She determine⌴ and non-negotiables and then slowly and quietly rebu⌴ from the inside out. I know many of you are reading this and cheering her on as you read. Some of you are reading this thinking, *How do I get there? I feel lost and alone, yet something within me is calling me to draw the line in the sand and begin walking this out step by step.* If that's you, we all say, "Welcome, and walk with us—the brave and the bold who choose to live renewed from the inside out every day."

To My Twenty-Year-Old Self

In every interview I conducted leading up to this book, I asked, "With what you know now, what would you say to your twenty-year-old self?" The responses were telling:

- Go to therapy earlier rather than later.

- You can have it all but not all at once.

- Don't compare, it will keep you hidden and kill your spirit.

- Don't grow up too fast. Don't get married so young.

- Don't lose yourself in someone else. You don't need anyone else to fulfill who you are.

- What you do is not who you are.

- You can design your life and accomplish anything.

- You're good enough. You are loved. Realize your worth.

- Don't listen to what people say. Don't get hung up on what others think, and don't follow the crowd.

- Be yourself. Be confident in who you are. This is who you're meant to be.

- Not everyone is going to like you and that's okay.

- Don't crave attention. Find authentic love in the right places. Hang in there; it gets better. It's all going to be okay.

These words contain valuable wisdom. If I were to thread it together and take all the sage wisdom from these beautiful souls and craft it into a few sentences to share with my kids, it would go something like this: You are enough, you are loved, and everything you are walking through will pass and get better. You are exactly who you're meant to be, so don't rush or crave attention. Don't be afraid because love is coming, and it will find you. True love wraps you up in a blanket and whispers, "I'm here." You are worth so much more than you can imagine, and although life may try and tell you that you aren't, trust me; you are enough. You are stronger than you know. Find someone wise and let them stand alongside you and teach you. Take risks and cherish moments. Don't rush to say, "I do," but meet people who will help refine you along the way. Let your hair down, lie on the grass, watch sunsets and sunrises, and gaze at the moon. Life will find you.

We all need voices like this to help us know that we have value simply because we are who we are. God made us a seed of who we were born to be, and the changes of life help us sprout, blossom, and grow into the fullness of who we are. This is beautiful, and you are beautiful.

A Letter to Ella (My Thirteen-Year-Old Daughter)

I want to be one of the voices speaking this wisdom into my children's lives. I want them to skip over the lessons I learned the hard way, so they can go further, love better, and live more fully. With that heart, I wrote this letter to my youngest daughter:

My sweet girl. Where do I start? You, my darling, are enough in every way. You don't need permission or approval from any-one to be exactly who you are meant to be, and who that is will be found in a journey of discovery that lasts a lifetime. Don't rush it; breathe in the moments whether they captivate your heart or tear it apart. The moments matter, and it's through the building of moments that minutes are formed, and from min-utes, hours, and from hours, days, and days turn into weeks and weeks into years.

I have loved my life. I have been hurt, abused, disregarded, and discarded. I have been seen as less than, stupid, ugly, and at times my worth has been ripped to shreds. In the same breath, I have been celebrated, loved, cherished, held close, and carried. I have loved deeply, and I have been loved deeply. The regrets I have are few, and I can only put that down to living fully, unbri-dled, and freely, and from learning to live in the present rather than being suffocated by the past or obsessing about the future. I see life through rose-colored glasses, and I hope you do too. Life is sweet, and it's waiting for you to explore every corner of it.

Exhale, sweet one. Don't hold on to life or things too tightly. Live life with your palms facing upward, open, and ready to re-ceive and give. Let people in; it's risky, and you might get hurt, but it's worth it. Show up and be fully yourself because the world needs you—wholeheartedly. Don't be afraid to love and be loved. Stand for truth and in your truth. Be kind because everyone you meet is fighting a battle you know nothing about.

When you're old enough, drink good wine and stay away from the cheap stuff; it will only give you a headache. Donate to good causes and do things just because. Listen to people and look them in the eye knowing that you will see God in them. Let them see God in you too.

I want you to know that like your siblings, you have always been wanted. The reason there is a gap of time between you and Gabriel is because it took us a little longer to have you. For whatever reason, God was teaching us patience at that time. It was hard because I wanted to meet you, to hold you, to know you.

From the moment you were born, you have had this spirit of sweetness about you; everyone could see it. You are kind, darling, and your kindness is gentle and meaningful. Parts of you mesmerize me: Your laugh always makes me smile, and I will never tire of hearing it. Your love for people is inspiring, and your search for justice is challenging. Your creativity will push boundaries; you have and always will see things before others. You will be moved by compassion, and that's a good thing.

Sweet girl, you are more than enough, and you are a carrier of light and love. Share it with the world. Be brave and know that my pompoms are strapped to my wrists. I am cheering you on now and forever.

A Practice from The Gathering Cloud
Retreating to Value Yourself

1. When was the last time you treated yourself—had a massage, a pedicure, or a night out to a movie?

2. Do something for yourself—alone or with someone whose company you enjoy. Loving yourself and showing value to yourself is important. Self-care is more than just the basics of food, water, and shelter, so get out there and do something for you. You are worth it!

how can I do that this week?

in my days off I will go into the city (w/ or w/out others) and I will visit a coffee shop + somewhere I have never been before.

7

FEAR IS A LIAR

Fear, he is a liar. He will take your breath,
stop you in your steps. Fear is a liar.
He will rob your rest, steal your happiness.
Cast your fear in the fire, 'cause fear, he is a liar.

—Zach Williams[22]

Lies trap us in fear, but what is fear really? I have a girlfriend who was going through a messy marriage situation. She was scared, felt alone, and had no idea what the future looked like. My heart had been breaking as I spent hours on the phone with her. One of her texts was so hard to read. It simply read: *Suze, I'm so scared.* Most of us can identify with that text in some way, shape, or form, so it's important to understand what fear is. Fear is False Expectations Appearing Real.

Let's start with false expectations. We don't know what could, will, or may happen in any situation. We can let our minds run wild and create a myriad of imagined expectations. I've heard it said: How would you treat a friend who lied to you as much as your fears have? The reality is that we have all spent far too much time worrying about things that never actually happened. Fear robs us of living fully.

Now, with all of that in mind, fear can be used for good. Although it rarely propels us forward, it can—if you let it. Once you boil fear down to false expectations appearing real, and you remind yourself of that, you can move forward. None of us know what outcomes lie ahead. We take risks every day without thinking about it. I'm confident that as I drive to the gym in the morning that I will make it there without having an accident, and that whilst at the gym my coordination will be on point, so I won't drop a barbell on my head.

Each one of us has these sorts of things we do that come with inherent risks, but they are just parts of our days, so we go about them with confidence that is built on past success. But in some cases (like writing this book), I do things even though I'm scared. In fact, whilst writing this book, if it wasn't for my family and friends, you wouldn't be reading it now. I have written every word with fear, but I haven't let fear hold me back. I've learned to respond to fear with faith, hope, and trust. Is this courage? I hope so.

Get Out of Your Own Way

Have you ever taken time to sit and ponder life? I mean have you *really* questioned why you do things a certain way? Why do you respond in ways that seem weird or frustrating to you? Why do you hesitate when an opportunity presents itself? Bravery examines our actions and reactions in a forensic way.

I find myself doing this a lot—especially now at forty-eight years old. I realize I respond to events and situations in established patterns. I've hit a point where I've said enough is enough. I don't want to live like this anymore, so I'm making steps to change patterns that have developed. It's quite astounding and freeing. I pleasantly surprise myself when I respond in a way that is new, or when I consciously lay down a past behavior and adopt or apply a new way to be. Not all that long ago, my husband and I were in a discussion that had an edge to it. At a certain point in the conversation, he pointed something out about me, and in an instant I recognized a patterned response of mine creeping in, but I chose to respond in a new way.

Not only did my new response shock my husband (I could tell by his look of surprise and confusion—and maybe a little joy), but my response also did something within me that felt *really* good. I realized I had gotten out of my own way by making room for truth with humility and honesty. Rather than letting hurt, frustration, and the desire to make my point dictate my actions, my response allowed for healing and healthy conversation to continue. It's hard to explain how liberating it felt.

You might be reading this thinking, *Come on, Susan, has it really taken you this long to figure this out?* It hasn't taken me this long to know this is the right way of doing things, but it has taken this long of a process for me to get out of my own way and actually *do* what was right.

I think we stand in our own way more often than not, and we miss opportunities, open doors, relationships, growth, and even love because we stand in our way. We need to take a good hard look at ourselves, and as I've said many times, be brave enough to acknowledge what's happening, what we need to do to move over, and how we can allow our true selves to live. I promise you the taste of that freedom will compel you to continue to be brave and to simply be.

The Forty-Year-Old Version of Me

We moved to Australia after 1997, when Hong Kong was given back to China from the British. I think my husband was craving wide open spaces, and Australia called, so we packed up and made our way down under to start anew. Then in 2007, change rang our doorbell again in the form of a business opportunity in Los Angeles, so we packed up three kids and moved across the ocean to North America. The business didn't happen like the dream had promised, so after a year of loving LA and Philip working crazy hours, we decided to move to Canada. It was bliss.

I was so happy to be home and living near family and life-long friends—and having four distinct seasons. I loved every moment of it. Our house was always bursting with guests, and I still believe that we lived on the most stunning street in all of Canada with the most extraordinary neighbors. Whispering Water Bend, it was named, and I still long to return to those days. Our memories made there will stay with me forever.

Change yet again rang our doorbell, and the opportunity to move back to Australia presented itself in 2013. Philip, eager to come back, helped bring us all across the line, and the decision was made to go. But along with our decision meant I had to announce the move to my family. Thus far, that has been one of the hardest things I've ever had to do.

When I had to tell my family, I realized that maybe the forty-year-old version of me wasn't as appealing as previous versions of me. You see, I think we can allow people to put us in boxes that make them comfortable, and we learn to live inside that box. We make decisions from that confined space, and we let the box begin to define us. We operate in a way that is foreign to the truth of who we are.

Perhaps you have been in a conversation with someone who said their family just doesn't know who they really are. Or perhaps you've been with a good friend in a new setting, maybe surrounded by their old friends or work colleagues, and all of a sudden they start acting in a way that seems out of character for them. The truth is they are behaving from the confines of the box they have been placed inside—the box from which they are known.

We easily become captives to who people think we are and what makes them comfortable, even if that means we live in a way that accommodates *their* feelings and desires above our own need to live out of our true self. We grow and change throughout life—and thankfully so. I'm so glad I'm not the person I was five years ago, ten years ago, or even three months ago. I, like many of you, choose to be on an ever-evolving path, so staying inside a box to make others comfortable just isn't an option.

When I told my family we were moving, it became apparent to me that maybe the forty-year-old version of me wasn't as appealing to them as the twenty or thirty-year-old version. I realized that staying in Canada could have meant staying inside the box and doing what made others comfortable. This meant our next step was an opportunity to grow once again, and it has been a substantial growth period for me, personally, perhaps one of the more soul-changing times in my life.

It has been hard, sad, and at times very lonely, and I still do long for Whispering Water Bend and the beauty that Canada offers, but I am grateful that I stepped out of the box and made a life-altering decision that has brought me to this moment of being.

Amplified Voices

So often in life, we are defined by other people's opinions of us or their desire for us to be a certain way. But my question is whose permission do you need to be yourself, and why do you need it? Have you given people voice into your life in a way that holds you back? Counsel is necessary but find those who have wisdom and believe in you—not those who see you as less than the person God says you are. I think we need to be aware of the voices that are the most amplified in our lives.

What's surprising is that the voice could be a teacher from the past—reminding us that we are no good, or that we'll never amount to anything. Or, on the contrary, it could be a teacher who believed in us and thought the world of us. It could be friends who are threatened by our success. It could be someone we've never met before, someone we've read about, or someone who inspires us and mentors us from afar. Who is speaking loudly to you? Who are you listening to?

Embracing Gratitude

Much of the fear we face is focused on outcomes, key performance indicators, and measurables. How is this project going to turn out? If we step out into that choice, will we get our desired result? Advertisers promise outcomes. Vacation destinations give the impression that all our woes will be solved if we spend a week and countless dollars at their establishment. Outcomes are everywhere.

What's interesting is that there are no guarantees. There are promises of a better tomorrow, fixes, lotions, and potions, but in the end, outcomes are often beyond our control. That's not to say we should be reckless. It's still true that usually a failure to plan is a plan to fail. But are we dependent on the outcomes going exactly as planned in order to have peace with our lives?

There's nothing wrong with wanting certain outcomes. I want a happy marriage and thriving children, and believe me, I'm working toward that end. But I've released the need to have that outcome in order to be at peace. Letting go of the need to have a certain outcome settles the fear that it won't happen, and it shifts our attention to what we're grateful for instead.

Breathe through the letting go, and as you let go of your emotional connection to the outcome, something deep within you will begin to happen. You will begin to shift your attention to what you're grateful for, and often your gratitude isn't even related to whatever is driving your desire for a certain outcome.

When we shift our attention, our emotional need follows, and gratitude rests in its place, which fills our tanks. Gratitude is a powerful yet underrated state of being. By letting go of the outcomes, we find ourselves in the present instead of the future. We begin to appreciate what is in us and around us. Fear, anxiety, and worry about the future diminish along with past should-haves and could-haves. It is out of gratitude that we begin to live in the present, as we appreciate the simple things right before us rather than grabbing and clinging to outcomes and longings that elude us.

Diana Butler Bass once wrote, "Gratitude is not about stuff. Gratitude is the emotional response to the surprise of our very existence, to sensing that inner light and realizing the astonishing sacred, social, and scientific events that brought each one of us into being. We cry out like the psalmist, 'I am fearfully and wonderfully made!'"[23]

I had the opportunity to attend a silent retreat held by my friend and mentor, Alicia Britt Chole. It was my first silent retreat, and although I was excited, I wasn't sure what to expect. I didn't know how I would possibly stay silent for days at a time. To my surprise, I fell in love with the experience. I began to find myself there, and I was overcome with gratitude.

The retreat is held on a beautiful property in Missouri. It was spring, so the ice and snow had melted but there was still a chill in the air. The property is riddled with places to rest and settle. Nestled in the trees are benches for those who want to sit, and there are hiking trails for the more active silent guest. As you follow one of the paths, it weaves through the dense trees and all the way down to the winding river, where there's a stunning deck on the water. Every day of the retreat I found myself drawn to the outdoors and down to that deck. I would sit and let the spring sun rest on my face, and I would breathe it all in.

This retreat reminded me of my love for nature and the outdoors. As a child, I spent most of my life in paddocks with my horse, or riding my bike through the streets calling out, "Look, Mom, no hands!" I loved the outdoors, and for whatever reason I had allowed myself to be pulled inside. Maybe it was work, the responsibility of family, or just the weight of life that caused me to stay inside. I realized I needed to bust out and get into the wide-open spaces I loved.

Since that retreat I have done just that. I have spent time in nature. I have discovered my love for walks, and I try to do at least three seven-kilometer hikes a week. I go by myself or with anyone who is interested in making their way up a mountain and down again. I have also discovered a renewed sense of gratitude whilst on these hikes. I find myself thanking God for the trees that give us oxygen, for the leaves on the trees, for the sun and the sky, for my family and friends, and for breath in my lungs. Gratitude has changed my heart and mind, and through gratitude I have discovered a peace I never knew. I am grateful for those days spent in silence by the side of the river.

Resting in God: Saanvi's and Aaradhya's Stories

Saanvi is a thirty-seven-year-old married woman with three boys. She lives in a remote village in India. I had the honor of speaking with her through a translator, and the conversation caused me to think deeply.

We spoke about life and her children, and I asked her what challenges she faced as a twenty-first century woman. Interestingly, the word challenge seemed to be a difficult one to translate. She didn't understand the word, and there didn't seem to be one we could translate properly, so we talked until we finally landed in a place where we both understood one another and allowed the conversation to flow.

She told me nothing was really difficult in her life and that her days were filled with normal activities, which included work and caring for her family. Her biggest concerns were how they would eat each day—how they would live and survive.

. Survival was her concern, but she didn't see it as a challenge; it was just part of her everyday life. She did struggle with loneliness, as her parents didn't live near her, and she missed them. Her husband was battling Dengue fever, so that was a concern for her, but she was choosing to trust God in all of this. Her default was not focusing on her concerns, but she told me that God keeps her, and she finds her peace there.

Aaradhya is a thirty-five-year-old mother of five children. She married at nineteen, and she has struggled her entire life thinking of herself as just a poor, weak woman. Through a translator, she told me about life and the concerns she had. One of her children, a son, was unwell, and the biggest concern for her was being able to buy his medicine, so he could stay well. Her husband was out of work, so the responsibility rested on her shoulders to not only work to pay for the medicine and their daily living expenses but to also care for the family as well. She worried every day about money and juggling the demands of life.

Interestingly, she too was unable to understand what I meant when I asked what her greatest challenge was in life. It just didn't make sense because she didn't see the responsibilities she had to carry as challenges. She was simply grateful they were all alive, and she could provide for them, and because of that she told me that she celebrates the days she has with her family.

These two women deal with concerns far more profound than what most of us will ever have to face, yet because of gratitude and resting in God, they don't consider their concerns as challenges. That is the power of gratitude and walking with God: It can lead us to overcome our fears no matter how challenging the circumstances may be.

A Practice from The Gathering Cloud
Retreating to Deal with Fear and Express Gratitude

1. Find a quiet spot where you won't be distracted for ten minutes.

2. Invite the Holy Spirit to wash over you, so you feel God's presence with you.

3. Recall a thought that you associate with some type of fear. Be aware of it and how it makes you feel.

4. Say quietly to yourself, "Let go," and as you do, let that thought go.

5. Bring to mind something that you are grateful for. Be aware of it and how it makes you feel. Now say quietly to yourself, "Thank you," and as you do, let that thought go.

6. Continue to alternate between a fearful thought and a grateful thought, using the words *let go* and *thank you* to let go of them.

7. Continue this until you want to end the practice.

8

RESILIENCE: RISE TO ADVERSITY

Someone said adversity builds character,
but someone else said adversity reveals character.
I'm pleasantly surprised with my resilience.
I persevere, and not just blindly. I take the best,
get rid of the rest, and move on, realizing
that you can make a choice to take the good.

—BROOKE SHIELDS[24]

I am continually blown away by what people walk through in life. I'm amazed, astonished, and completely captivated by stories of resilience. Where does resilience come from? Is it something related to God?

Many, if not most people, are walking around carrying incredible hurt and pain, and the fact that they get up every morning and keep going through it all is crazy to me. Most of us don't have the luxury of sitting on the couch and waiting for our circumstance to pass.

Resilience looks different for everyone, but it's there for all of us. Sometimes we don't even recognize resilience because we just keep going, and it isn't until we stop and reflect that we realize just how resilient we are.

The Beauty of Resilience

I find myself fascinated with how we keep going. Where do we find the strength? What keeps us moving forward when everything seems to shout at us to stop, give up, and let go?

After my father passed away, my mother lived in their big home all alone. It remained a vibrant place for family gatherings, but as she got older, the property began to feel unmanageable. She didn't want to leave, but I think deep down she knew change was in the air. The time had come for us to find a place for her that didn't require so many demands and allowed her the opportunity to live independently but in community.

I liken the place we found to living on a cruise ship. They have activities, meals, dancing, outings, and more. You name it, they have it. While we were touring the facility, my sister and I were envious and tempted to grab a unit for ourselves. It was that good. To help my mom through this transition and stay true to our family culture, we gathered around the dining table to have a tough conversation. My mother is a very strong woman. She's kind, smart, and has a great sense of humor. Her style is impeccable, and she has always been fiercely independent. A conversation like this wasn't going to be easy.

I watched my mother as she listened. I can't imagine what it felt like for her to hear all the changes that needed to happen. Imagine having to look at your life and know that everything was about to change dramatically. She was going to lose her independence not only by giving up her huge home, but also her privacy by moving into a community of what she deemed "old people." The life of independence she had always known was coming to an end, and she couldn't do anything to stop it. At one point during our conversation, tears started to flow. My mother excused herself from the table, asked for a moment to compose herself, and walked away with her face in her hands. My heart crumbled.

I was definitely the weakest link at the table. My brother and sister had warned me that I needed to stay the course and not allow emotion to change my position. It was hard. I just wanted to cave in to avoid seeing my mother in this state. She returned to the table, and I saw the beautiful resilience my mother had shown us our entire lives.

Over the years, this strong woman lived resiliently. When she was pregnant with my eldest brother, Robert, my father had his first heart attack at twenty-six years old. They were a young couple about to welcome their first child into the world, and her husband lay on a gurney, fighting for his life. Pregnant and scared, she rose resilient. Before I was born, I had a brother who died as a baby. She rose resilient. My older brother, Robert, and my sister, Katherine, saw her emerge from the depths of that pain. I had the opportunity to see her resilience when my little brother, Peter, was diagnosed with Down Syndrome. She rose again resilient and created an integrated life for him that was unprecedented.

I saw her resilience emerge when my father lay on another gurney, prepped for a major surgery, and she said what could have been her final farewell. I saw it again at his funeral when she finally did say farewell to the man she had loved since she was fourteen. In the days, weeks, months, and years that followed, I watched resilience unfold as she carried on and parented us through the loss of our father.

Here we were again witnessing her resilience as she graceful-ly said, "It looks like this is the plan, and I just have to go with it." Watching her resilience was astounding to me. Did she realize that she was again offering us a gift? Did she know she was still teaching us how to live well? Did she know how strong she was in that moment?

I'm not sure of any of those things, but what I do know is resilience truly is a woman's best strength. There was so much beauty and grace displayed around the table on that cold, Canadian night. As a family we came together and had a tough conversation that was made easier because my mother learned and lived the art of resilience, and once again, she rose.

Resilience in the Darkest of Days: Deborah's Story

Where do I begin to tell Deborah's story? She was a thirty-one-year-old mother living her dream with her small family of three little ones and hope for more children. The day they found out she was pregnant with their fourth child was exciting for this young couple. Their hopes and dreams were coming to pass.

I knew immediately there was something very captivating about this girl. There was a depth to her that intrigued me. She was young, fresh-faced, and beautiful, and it was a beauty that comes from deep within. Her words were well crafted, and as she spoke about her kids and husband, there was a richness in her voice.

She started telling me about her fourth pregnancy because that's when everything changed for her. During one of her routine checkups, it was discovered she had cancer. From that point on, everything about the pregnancy changed very quickly, and this young couple suddenly faced decisions no one should have to make. Questions like: Do they continue with the pregnancy? Does she do the recommended chemotherapy, or does she go through the next months with rapidly failing health—risking both her life and the life of the baby? How do you make decisions like this? It wasn't meant to be like this at all.

She talked about her husband, and how he really pulled around her during this time. She was scared, there was no question, but once they made their decisions and had a plan in place, she said she rose resilient in the face of fear, loss, devastation, heartache, pain, and even death. This thing called resilience shows up in the most desperate of moments, puts a rod in our backs, and causes us to stand when it looks like we should crumble.

The decision wasn't an easy one, but with all the facts in their hands, coupled with their faith, they chose chemotherapy. At twenty-two weeks pregnant, Deborah sat in a hospital chair and began her first of four rounds of chemo.

She was desperate to be there for her children, and through the pain of everything both physically and emotionally she relied on the strength of God, her husband, the joy and love of her children, and the support of her community to carry her through. Despite being scared, she asked God for peace to cover her anxiety, so that even through all of this her children would see their mother happy and brave.

Deborah shared about the encounters she had with God throughout all of this. There were the conversations she had with a dear aunt who was a woman of faith, and a conference she attended where she heard messages of healing. She began to devour teachings and listen to things that built her faith and gave her hope. It became apparent where this depth that I recognized came from—the timbre in her voice, the eyes that smiled with a sense of knowing.

The day we chatted was a "good day" for her. She was wearing her headscarf to cover her balding head. She had recently had her eyebrows tattooed (and they were on point), and she was feeling good. It was apparent that the work being done in and through her was not only on a cellular level but also a deep inner working of the soul. I will never forget the conversation we had that day. We ended with my asking if I could pray for her. It was powerful for both of us. Perhaps it was a divine moment in time.

I'm happy to report that her sweet little miracle was born and is healthy, vibrant, and unharmed by the decisions she had to make for both of them. She remains well, and cancer is a distant memory, but the woman who emerged from that journey is one who I want on my side if I'm ever in a fight for my life. She has faced death, found resilience in the darkest of days, and she rose.

Resilience in the Face of Pain: Laurie's Story

Laurie is a fifty-year-old woman who was raised in what she could only describe as a very dysfunctional family. There were seven children in desperate need of parental care, love, and support, but sadly, it didn't exist. They only received abuse and pain.

Her life was complicated and had layers that were almost indescribable. As a young girl, her mother left the family, leaving them even more exposed and vulnerable. Her father stayed and gave what he could to be who the children needed him to be— both mother and father, but the absence remained.

Mystery still surrounds her mother's decision to leave, but with the years that have passed the reason is almost insignificant. Now forty years later, this stunning woman stood poised with beauty and dignity. Tears filled her eyes as she told me how her aging mother has returned into her life, and her mother's care has landed on Laurie's shoulders.

Laurie is now responsible for her mother who had abused her both physically and mentally. Now in her final years, with years of unmet dreams and unrealized relationship between them, this woman was asked to find the love for her mother that she once had, but a love that had become riddled and tainted with buried pain, rejection, and loss. She found resilience in the face of pain. She chose to care for her mother—scars and all, and she rose.

Remember How I Taught You to Walk and Talk

There is a well-traveled video on Facebook of an aging woman who wrote a letter to her children asking them to be kind to her as she ages. In the letter, she reminds her children of the times she helped them tie their shoes, how she repeatedly answered their questions of "why," and how she was gentle whenever they made mistakes. She writes this to them because as she's aging, she's forgetting how to do things, and she's becoming more dependent. She compels them to remember who she once was and asks them to show her the same kindness. The video is a tearjerker, and it gets me every time.

Could life really go that way for any of us? Will we really come to a time when our parents can't keep up? Will they forget us? What will that be like? And how does one cope through that? Resilience, friends. We will do it with pure resilience and the constant reminder that this is the person who taught you to walk and talk.

During those seasons of life, it is especially important to remember that while we once used to depend on our parents for just about everything, we have now learned to depend on God instead. Just as we don't look to our husbands or our children, we also don't look to our parents. When we know God is the One who's looking after us, it helps us to let go of our parents with grace, so we can, in turn, help meet their needs, as they once met ours.

Resilience in Superhuman Care: Katherine's Story

This story comes from close to home for me, literally. This is the story of the resilient woman who is my sister, Katherine, who cares not only for our aging mother but also our forty-two-year-old brother who has Down Syndrome. Days are challenging, and there are times when Katherine truly feels like her life should be documented for television. Being so far away and unable to help is a challenge I grapple with daily. For the most part, I am a sounding board and someone to share the hilarious moments with, though at times someone to sob with as well.

None of it is easy, and with a growing family of her own and a busy career, she is truly caught in the press trying to keep everything and everyone intact—including herself. My sister falls into the "sandwich generation," a term given to those who are sandwiched between caring for both their parents and their children simultaneously. Although my mother and brother don't live with her, they do live in the same city, and their needs are significant.

My sister has always been one of the kindest people I know. If I were to guess, her love language would be acts of service, and in providing acts of service she can't be faulted. Resilience is something she wears extraordinarily well. The care she provides for my mother, brother, and her own family requires superhuman power.

Life for my sister and others like her is exhausting. At the end of the day, when most of us kick our shoes off and collapse onto the couch, people like my sister are probably running errands for the extra people in their care. I know Fridays are a big day for my sister. She works, manages her youngest daughter's schedule, supports her two eldest children who are in college, and she supports her husband. What's added to her Friday experience is my little brother's need for his Friday treats, which means a trip to the supermarket to buy one chocolate bar, one can of coke, and one bag of chips. This is his routine, and it cannot be messed with, so amidst the busyness of my sister's week, she has to fit in even more. That's not to mention our mom's weekly blood work and the rest of the list I haven't mentioned.

For Katherine and others in the sandwich generation, the emotional, physical, and at times financial weight can cause even further challenges that extend into their personal health, the well-being of their own families, depression, and career development. The resilience these caretakers show is extraordinary.

It's said that everyone has resilience hardwired into them; it's just a matter of tapping into it. For my sister, could it be that her ability to cope in this trying time has a lot to do with the strength of her relationships both near and far? Clearly, she would benefit from someone lightening the load and helping her in the day-to-day, but in the absence of that option, do the rest of us still play a part in walking this out and helping them remain resilient?

Katherine reminds me to never underestimate what it means to be on the other end of the phone line or FaceTime—to stay connected regardless of distance or awkwardness. We need to push through and support one another in whatever capacity we can. Over the course of the last two years, as the needs of my mother and brother have increased, I have battled with the angst of living away from home. I can't change that at the moment, but what I can be is present. Even in my physical absence, I can show up and be present for all that is happening. Every day I wish I was taking my mom to her appointments or my brother out to lunch. I wish I could sit with my sister and laugh about the craziness of life, so in that I too have to find resilience. We both rise.

Find Your Suzie

This is for all the young moms out there who are desperate to find meaning amidst stretch marks, temper tantrums, lack of sleep, cracked nipples, and a little (or a lot of) extra weight that just won't shift. Where does resilience come from?

That's a hard one, and I'm not going to sugarcoat anything. It truly is a magical time of life, but there is no denying that it is hard. I would suggest it may be even harder now than it was when my kids were little because minute by minute you are bombarded with Instagram images that depict perfectly sleeping toddlers, lunches that make even the most celebrated chef green with envy, decorated bedrooms that rival the greatest Pinterest post, and sexy-night-out shots with "the love of my life," when all you want to do is crawl into a hole and sleep for a week. I get it. I was there. I've lived it, and I know the feeling well.

The road to resilience, in this case, is interesting because it's paved with speed bumps along the way. But don't be dismayed; it can be found. For me, resilience in this season of life was found through an older friend. My friend, Suzie, was a lifeline during these years. Her three kids were older than mine, and she provided much-needed perspective. She offered a place to collapse onto the couch if needed, babysitting when desperate, and countless dinners when I couldn't cope or didn't want to. I've told her on many occasions how she impacted my life and our collective lives by keeping me sane and merely being my friend.

Resilience in this season comes in and through the most unexpected relationships. Once again, infrastructure is core to resilience, so make the necessary choices to build this into your life. Firstly, find your Suzie—someone who will help you stay sane and bring clarity when nothing makes sense and who will hold you up when you're at the end of your tether.

Then *be* someone's Suzie. Be the infrastructure they need. Learn the wisdom to understand that there are times to be your friend's shoulder to cry on and times to be the foot that kicks them in the butt. Wherever you find yourself on your journeys with your friends, walking with them through the highs and lows of life will always remind you that joy is to be celebrated on the other side of hardship.

Watching one another's resilience shine through may be all you need to recognize your own. Either way, life is unquestionably easier with a good friend. Remember, when you're on top of the world there is wine and cheese to be had, but when things seem bleak, don't worry, with friends there is always wine, cheese, tissues, and lots of chocolate.

Also, never forget your connectedness to God, the source of life that will always draw you higher. This is the ultimate resilience.

Resilience through Perimenopause and Menopause

This almost seems like an oxymoron. How on God's green earth are we meant to find anything during this season of life, much less resilience? But alas, I've come to know, as have many of you and those I interviewed, that this season of life requires us to possibly be the most resilient ever.

I recall sitting in my doctor's office, and I think my opening line after she politely asked how she could help was, "I feel like the wheels of the bus have come off, and I'm losing my mind." That was quickly followed by my request (or more specifically a plea) for a hysterectomy. Extreme measures are taken as we travel through these unstable years, which can extend into a decade and beyond, and that, my friends, is the reason resilience in this season is paramount.

Whether it be embarrassing flooding, outrageous outbursts, excessive sweating, or the constant tricks your memory plays on you, this season is hard. Thankfully, we now talk about all of this. I think back to my mother when she was going through this stage. Women of her generation didn't talk about things like we do now. Instead, they suffered through everything without even the support of their own mothers. Everything seemed to be so hush-hush in their day, and we have flipped the tables and now can be guilty of the overshare.

In the overshare, we seem to find that resilience carries us through. The older generation found it as well. I'm not sure how or where, but I do know that our current infrastructure offers us the opportunity to talk to our friends about some of the more challenging life experiences, and as a society we recognize mental health issues and the impact our hormones have on our emotional and physical being.

Thankfully, I was able to sit in my doctor's office and express my concern about the bus, which was, in fact, a concern about my mental health and wellness. A conversation with my doctor and blood tests coupled with meditation and being kind to myself have helped me find resilience. It doesn't mean that this stage of life is easy. On the contrary, I'm finding it to be one of the most challenging. But life goes on, and every day is different. Sometimes I feel like there are no wheels, and sometimes I feel fully in control and content.

Thank you to my doctor and to all my girlfriends who embrace the overshare for what it is. In and through each one of you, I'm finding my resilience, staying the course, and being true to myself. Resilience carries us through and gets us to the next stage. We rise.

A Practice from The Gathering Cloud
Retreating to Encourage Resilience

1. Find a quiet place or a place connected to nature.

2. Think of a time in the past, perhaps in your early childhood, when you were innocent, feeling completely safe with an overwhelming sense of joy. It may bring a smile to your face with memories of happiness and fun.

3. Now think about yesterday. Dwell on the things that occurred, the places you went, the things you did, the things you didn't do, what you said, what was said to you, what you thought and felt. You may be considering whether it was a good day or a bad day. Emotions or feelings may come up. Now raise your hands as if to offer something to God and say, "The past is gone." Hold that position for a few seconds and then bring your hands down to your lap.

4. Now think about tomorrow. Dwell on the things that you expect to happen and the things you have to do. You may feel some worry, fear, or anxiety, or maybe anticipation and excitement. Now raise your hands as if to offer something to God and say quietly, "God, I give you the future that is yet to come." Hold that position for a few seconds and return your hands to your lap.

5. Finally, be aware of the present—where you are, why you are here, and how you are here. Lift your hands to God and say, "Thank you, God, for the life I have. Because you are with me, I am strengthened to overcome all that comes my way."

9

BEAUTY FROM ASHES

We know what we are, but not what we may be.

—William Shakespeare[25]

My family always went to church together. Every Sunday morning, we were up and out the door. The small town I grew up in had only nine hundred people, yet within that prairie town were four churches of four different denominations. Our family and most of our relatives attended the same church. I remember those days well because it was back when church bells would ring, and I loved the sound. Each church had their own bell, and the bells would echo throughout our quaint town. It was like a declaration, a joyous sound for all to hear.

I remember sitting on the hard wooden pews and doing my best to listen to the sermon. I liked our minister. He was a kind man, and his words always seemed to land somewhere in my heart even as a young child. Sitting on those pews, however, was a challenge. My church had five exquisite stained-glass windows that told a biblical story by piecing together different shapes and pieces of glass. Every church had their own stained-glass stories to tell. The richness and beauty filled this young girl, teen, and eventually woman with the sensation of life.

Stained glass is beautiful in any form. It was originally used in medieval times both to enhance the beauty of churches and to teach biblical stories or doctrines through narrative or symbolism. During this time, churches were the center for learning in society. Although most people were illiterate, they could understand the story of God nearly in its entirety. The stories depicted in the works of glass formed the most stunning "books" ever written. Stained glass helped churches remain inclusive to everyone in the congregation—regardless of their education, so all could worship and understand God.

Masterpieces in the Making: Amanda's Story

Just like the cut pieces of glass that come together to form a masterpiece, the cut up, painful pieces of our lives can do the same. Amanda's story is a great example of that, but I warn you that it's a difficult story to read. If you have a history of abuse or are sensitive to stories of abuse, you may want to use extra caution in reading her story.

Amanda shared her story with me before one of our Get-RealLive Retreats. It was riddled with rejection after rejection, pain, the most horrific rape, verbal and physical abuse, and the list went on. I had never heard anything like it in my life, and I've heard a lot. It was awful. As I listened to her, I honestly did whatever I could to stop my tears. I literally had to remind my face to remain calm. I could hardly believe what I was hearing.

The pain this woman had endured was so evident in her life it was almost as if she walked with a heavy, saturated blanket over her. She never smiled. She could hardly look anyone in the eye. She was suspicious of everyone and kept most everyone at arm's length. Amanda was thirty-five years old and struggling to express love to her husband and her children. She didn't want to be touched nor did she want to touch. The abuse left her broken in ways I had never seen.

She spoke of times as a child where she felt she was literally running for her life, and times she stood in front of a fist to protect her siblings. She told stories of her mother being grabbed by the hair, and her head bashed into a table over and over. She recalled a dinner where her father leaned over the table and punched her brother in the face. Sexual abuse occurred within the family too. This is just a glimpse of the tragic physical violence and abuse Amanda endured. Because of everything Amanda had been through, she considered herself damaged goods—unworthy of anyone's time. She sincerely believed her breath was wasting what could better serve others.

As she shared her truth with me, all I could see was a stained-glass window. I could see beauty through her brokenness, and I could see that in and through it all, if she allowed a process to happen, the pieces could come together into something beautiful. On the last day of our retreat, I woke early and settled into the kitchen for a hot coffee and to enjoy the sights and sounds of the early morning. In walked this beautiful woman holding the tracksuit pants she'd worn throughout the entirety of the retreat. She sat down with me, and having apparently determined I could be trusted during the time of the retreat, words began to fall out.

When hosting retreats like this, my team and I understand that people come with a lot of pain. We understand how hard it can be to trust people you may not know. Thankfully, we were able to create a safe environment for her to share. As she spoke, I wept. I wept for the little girl. I wept for the teenage girl who hid away from the world; for the woman who desperately wanted to love her husband and craved intimacy but couldn't find it; for the mother who ached to love her kids and show them love. I wept at her courage and resilience despite such pain.

She bravely told her story and shared her truth. All the hurt, pain, and horror she had walked through was resurfacing, and by doing so she was beginning to own her story. Without even realizing it, she had given herself permission to begin the healing process from the inside out. Watching this experience of hers unfold before my eyes was stunning. In her mess and pain, she was absolutely beautiful.

As she shared the most painful memories of her life experience, somehow she began to smile. That wet, heavy blanket was peeled back, and her sorrow was replaced with a beauty that can only be described as joy. She had the most beautiful smile and eyes that danced like the stars in the sky.

When she finished sharing her story she looked down at the track pants neatly folded on her lap. She told me she was going to burn them because they had been her uniform, her safety net for twenty years. Tracksuit pants were her way of not drawing attention to herself—both wanted attention from her husband and kids and unwanted attention from people who could hurt her. They had been her shield to the world, her barrier to feelings. But it was time to let them go, and she wanted to burn them. You could hear the mixture of excitement and anxiety in her voice.

Later in the day, I saw her walk down to the fire. All alone and in her own time, she did what she needed and wanted to do. As she threw those pants into the fire, strength enveloped her. She came back to the house and told everyone what she had done. As she opened up and shared her truth, her internal mosaic was rebuilt, and the old was burned away. The fragments of her life, the shards of pain and shattered dreams were pulled together to form something more beautiful than before. I will never forget that conversation and what I witnessed.

Our pain bruises and batters us, and the stain and fragmentation it leaves can come together to form something stunning— if we allow it. Our truth can heal us, and our inner mosaic can begin to take form.

Broken Bones

Our second child, Gabriel, broke his arm when he was four years old. He was (and remains) an adventurous child, always discovering, pushing boundaries, and walking on the edge. What a life he has had and will continue to live; one filled with adventure and wonder. I admire his inquisitive nature, and his hunger for adventure.

The day he broke his arm was a beautiful day in Australia. We were out for a walk, and Gabriel decided to run through a grassy space nearby. With arms stretched out, pretending to be an airplane flying through the sky, he weaved his way through knee-high grass. He was putting all his effort into flying, and his little legs were running as fast as they possibly could. Laughing and gasping for air, he pushed on through the dips and turns until he hit one that was a little lower than the others. This caused his rhythm to change and—BOOM!—he was head over heels and rolling in the grass. I ran toward him thinking he would have knocked his teeth out or something but never expected what I saw.

I scooped him up from the ground, ready to dust him off and check him over, but as I gathered him up, I noticed his little arm was broken in two. What was once a straight, functioning arm had snapped into a v-shaped limb. It was awful to look at.

After hours in the emergency room and one surgery later, Gabriel was returned to us groggy and with a cast in place. The doctor explained to us that although he suffered a severe break, they were able to repair it. Then he told us something that surprised us: He said when we break a bone and have it repaired and reset, it becomes stronger than it was originally.

Not only was Gabriel's arm going to be okay and he would have full usage, but it was also going to be stronger than it was before. The break and the repair made him stronger. The pain he had to endure and the healing process he would have to walk through all made his bone stronger and more resilient. I found this fascinating.

Could our lives be like this? Could the innermost parts break yet heal stronger than before? Like Gabriel's broken bone, we may need painful reconstruction surgery. When something breaks, we need to allow it to be reset and then allow the process of healing to take place. In the case of Gabriel's arm, healing required a cast to keep it both in position and still; it took time and patience.

A broken heart will heal differently than a broken arm that we can see and touch. A spiritual break will also be different. Whatever the pain or break may be, the attention required to heal will be different, but it all begins with the first step, which is acknowledging and accepting that something isn't right.

Let's take a moment to think about this. Imagine if I had scooped Gabriel up, dusted him off, noticed his broken arm, but told him that he would be okay and should just get on with his day. Gabriel would have lived in agony—both short term and long. He would have become a different person because the physical pain he was feeling would have occupied most of his energy. He would have had to learn to hide the pain by ignoring it, medicating it, or becoming angry and taking his pain out on others. If allowed to heal without being properly reset, the break would have caused permanent deformity and potential loss of function. We see how necessary it is to acknowledge the broken-ness in a physical wound, but it is no less necessary with inner wounds.

Gabriel needed to be brave so that his arm could repair. Then, he needed to embrace the time it took to heal, so he could once again use his arm stronger and better than before. He need-ed to embrace and trust the process of healing, as scary as it was for a little four-year-old. He needed to trust the surgeon and his parents as he inhaled the anesthesia. He needed to let go and al-low the process to do exactly what it was meant to do: heal him.

In our lives, it's easier to sweep things under the carpet. To say we've been hurt internally is strangely seen as weak or needy.

To be honest about our health and well-being is almost taboo for some reason. Maybe it's because the level of inner hurt many of us have experienced goes beyond the Band-Aid level of emotional boo-boos that an average person knows how to treat. When I saw my son's arm, I knew I didn't have the expertise to deal with it; I needed a doctor. But a stigma persists for needing a doctor to heal inner wounds—despite the fact that emotional and psychological wounds are just as real and just as important to heal as physical ones.

It could also be that everyone is dealing with something of their own, so it's hard to take on someone else's hurt too. But I think that's just it: We're dealing with it rather than acknowledging, releasing, and embracing a process of healing. Dealing with things makes me think of control, like we're trying to wrangle something or force it into the right shape. Being brave and embracing a process seems much more like letting go and opening up, so that a journey can unfold.

Is it scary and vulnerable to open yourself up? Absolutely. Like Gabriel going to the operating table, healing is a place where we allow ourselves to go, and in that vulnerability, we allow a deep work to begin. In the resetting of thoughts and ideas, we acknowledge the pain, sadness, loss, depression, and physical hurt, and we begin the sometimes-slow journey of healing.

Like a broken arm, we can be rebuilt from the inside out. Imagine a life stronger and able to withstand more simply because of the trauma we've experienced. Could that pain become beauty? Yes, it can.

Let Go and Let God

Since I was a young girl, I've always had a profound understanding that at the helm of life was something much bigger than me. When times have been tough, I've certainly hoped and prayed that something grander than myself is directing this life I live. If I had to rest in the knowledge that I'm it—that the buck stops with me, and I had nowhere to rest and recline—I think I would crumble.

Let go and let God is an act of surrender, trust, and love. It is not an act of giving up. It's the opposite. We let go of our cares and burdens to a loving God. We do not deny that we have them. We acknowledge them, we experience them, but we do not need to live there. With open hands and open hearts, we let go. We let go with intention and consent to God's action and presence within us.

Sometimes this seems difficult to people who have been hurt. They want to know where God was when they were suffering. I could never answer that question, but I am inspired by stories like Amanda's because I can so clearly see God's work in her life—redeeming her from the brokenness of her past and creating something more beautiful. Without God, we would simply be stuck with our pain and brokenness, but because of God we can heal more strongly and beautifully than ever before. This is God's goodness to us that inspires us to trust. God is with us through it all. We are never alone.

A Practice from The Gathering Cloud
Retreating to See the Possibility of Beauty

1. Find a quiet place in nature where you can sit for ten minutes.

2. Close your eyes and say, "God, I welcome your presence here with me."

3. Think of the "ashes" in your life. It's okay to feel sadness over this loss.

4. Think of something beautiful that can come from your ashes. For example, where you have received comfort, you can comfort. Where you have received strength, you can strengthen. Dream what these ashes can become in God's redemptive hands.

5. Express gratitude to God and say, "May these dreams fulfill their purpose in your time."

10

SOMETIMES IT JUST HAS TO BE
WELL WITH YOUR SOUL

When peace like a river attendeth my way,
When sorrow, like sea billows roll,
Whatever my lot, Thou hast taught me to say,
"It is well, it is well, with my soul."

—HORATIO G. SPAFFORD[26]

You've heard me say throughout this book that life can be hard. No doubt about it, life is challenging. I remember a particularly challenging day that changed my perspective on life in a profound way. Let me first set the context for that day. At the time, Philip and I had two children: Sophia, who was three, and Gabriel, who was ten months. A few weeks earlier, Gabriel had just hit the nine-month mark, and I found myself dreadfully tired. It was strange because he was a good sleeper, which meant I was sleeping, enjoying motherhood, and adapting to two children quite well. But when he was nine months old, I began to feel overcome with fatigue.

I could hardly stay awake during the day. My energy levels were zapped, and I became a zombie at night. I remember talking to my mom about this. I told her how exhausted I was. In her wisdom, she gently asked, "Do you think you could be pregnant?"

I replied with a whimsical laugh, "Ha, not a chance. You have to do certain things for that to happen."

We laughed and ended our conversation, but as I put the phone down, I jolted upright with a faint memory that had been blurred by seemingly endless diaper changes and feedings for my growing son—maybe I could be pregnant after all.

I called Philip for clarity. His response to my somewhat vague questions caused my spine to straighten again—it was very possible that I was pregnant! There I was, holding my ten-month-old, babbling, sweet boy in my arms, reconciling in my mind the fact that I was, indeed, pregnant. Pregnant. This wasn't meant to happen. It wasn't part of our plan. How was this going to work? The processing quickly began in my mind, the reevaluating of life, and soon enough I was settled, and my heart content.

On a sunny day in March, I was busy in the house—doing the daily chores, making beds, hanging out the washing, and tidying up the house. Sophia was at preschool, and Gabriel was nestled in for his afternoon nap. Life felt good and right. I was still in the tired stages of my first trimester of pregnancy but was taking advantage of the burst of energy that I had.

I remember the moment everything changed like it was yesterday—the twinge in my stomach and the sharp piercing pain. I was standing beside a dresser in Gabriel's room and putting his tiny clothes away. I sat down and took a few deep breaths, and something just didn't seem right. I went to the bathroom and realized things were about to change. There was blood, and I knew in my gut that it wasn't minor pregnancy spotting.

I crawled into my bed and held my tummy. Gripped with fear and sheer panic at the height of discovering what was happening, I reached for the phone and called my sister, Katherine. When she answered, I burst into a flood of tears and said, "I'm bleeding, Katherine. I'm bleeding! This can't be happening!"

My sister responded with confidence, kindness, and gentle strength. She said seven words that not only changed my heart on that day of great sadness and loss, but those words have also impacted the way I have lived ever since. As my wailing turned to sobs, she heard me. She listened to the pain, the fear, the uncertainty, the anxiety, and the depths of my sadness, and she simply said, "Let it be well with your soul."

It was like God instantly invaded my space. I had a deeper understanding of what was about to happen, but I also knew it would be okay. My soul resonated with words that transcended language—words that held power; words that spoke to the innermost part of me: *let it be well with your soul.*

Everything was crumbling around me. My heart was breaking. My womb was rejecting my baby. But something more significant was reaching into my innermost being and calling forth life through the pure art of being: letting it be well with my soul—not fighting or striving, but merely allowing what needed to be actually *be.* It was well with my soul.

I've come to learn that we aren't in control, and sometimes we just need to let it be well with our souls. Part of us wants to pray against and believe it's not going to happen, but my reality was that I was miscarrying. As I embraced the reality instead of fighting it, peace invaded my heart; my mind and my ability to cope and walk through the pain of that day and the days, weeks, and years ahead changed because of it.

I remember the ride to the hospital. I was in so much pain. Having had three children and understanding the pain of childbirth itself, I can say this pain was greater than my hardest labor. It was a different pain, and one I can't really put into words, but the physical pain was almost unbearable. When we arrived at the hospital, I was rushed to my doctor. He performed an ultrasound and informed me that I was, indeed, losing my baby.

But what he discovered on that day was that I wasn't only losing one baby; in fact, I was pregnant with twins, and I was losing two babies. During the examination process, one baby did miscarry, but the ultrasound showed the other baby still in my womb. With tears flooding my eyes, I asked my doctor if maybe the other might survive and be okay. I was grasping for hope.

My doctor, a sweet man, held my hand, sat beside me on the bed, and told me that the other baby, although still in my womb, was already gone. It was now a matter of extraction. My hope shattered. It's said that hope deferred makes the heart sick. My hope was deferred but bouncing through my mind were the seven words my sister had said to me: "Let it be well with your soul." Overcome with profound sadness, I chose to let it be well with my soul.

Years later and there isn't a day that goes by that I don't think of those two sweet babies who never took their first breaths. They are part of me and I them. Who knew that I would have six children over the course of my life? I have the honor of walking through life with three of them, and three more are nestled in the recesses of my heart and soul. I never got to hold them or hear their voices, but I had the opportunity to carry them for a short time. It is well with my soul, and sometimes it has to be.

We Are Multidimensional

I think we often forget that we are body, soul, and spirit, and all three aspects of our lives require attention. I've often wondered what it would be like if we were able to look in the mirror and see our soul and spirit? What would we see? When we are physically unfit and unhealthy, we notice weight gain, bulges, and bumps. What would a healthy soul and spirit look like, and what would a sick or unhealthy one show?

How do we care for our soul and spirit? How do we live—body, soul, and spirit? I recently had the opportunity to have lunch with a woman named Tania Harris. Tania teaches people how to hear the voice of God. She was telling me that when she works with people and helps them tune their ears to listen to that voice, most times people will say to her that they've known that sound all their lives. They recognize it and realize that it has, in fact, been there whispering, guiding, correcting, and challenging them their entire life. What if we all tuned into that and began to live in a way that listens?

Over the last few years, I have embraced this spiritual practice. I've always been aware of my spirit and soul, but I realized that my experience was more a Sunday deal with a few prayers and readings scattered throughout the week. Mind you, those scatterings were more like a check-the-box kind of situation when I did what I thought was right and made sure I invited God into my week, rather than merely having a pleasant experience on a Sunday.

In 2015 though, I distinctly recall God telling me to be quiet, to listen, and to be still. It was then that I embarked on a journey of spiritual practice that has begun to shape my life in new and exciting ways. Through this practice, I have learned to live more by spirit than physical being alone. I wish I had a before and after picture that I could share, but that's not available beyond physical things. Instead, I take people on a journey with me.

Being multidimensional, we are, in fact, like the most beautiful of symphonies you've ever heard, which is why it is imperative that we care for ourselves holistically. Take some time to consider what your sound would be. Would it be captivating? Inspiring? It's like the question: "What would be the soundtrack to your life?" Well, what would the soundtrack to your being be?

Having lived in Hong Kong for many years, I had many opportunities to listen to Chinese opera, and I must admit it's not my favorite sound. I would hope my sound wouldn't resemble the Chinese opera. But there is a band called The Brilliance who have an instrumental song called, "You Are My Rescue," and it's a song I hope would be the expression of my multidimensional self. It's rich, bold, and it has depth. There is sadness and wisdom wrapped in the notes. It feels, and it's full of motion, hope, and joy. Could it be the song of my soul? What's your song?

We have a body, soul, and spirit. We must live in our spirit, and I would suggest that a grand mark of maturity is someone who lives by God's Spirit. We need to hear the voice of God and follow his Spirit instead of just following feelings and desires. Renew your mind each day by taking time to still yourself.

Speak to Your Soul

One question I'm often asked is: "Where does your confidence come from?" I find it a fascinating question because I guess it's just always been there. If I am to look back at my life, I would say it has a lot to do with my family and the life I was born into.

I had a brother who died before I was born. His name was Anthony, and he died of Sudden Infant Death Syndrome (SIDS) while my grandmother was looking after him. I've always marveled at the way my mother was able to walk through that. She didn't blame but gave the gift of forgiveness to her mother; that has always captivated me. Not that it was my grandmother's fault at all, but I can appreciate the pain and suffering my mom experienced and perhaps even feeling the need to assign blame.

After losing a child and a sibling, you can only imagine that I was wanted by my whole family. My birth carried healing and hope into a broken family who had mourned a profound loss. Their mourning turned to dancing; God gave them a gift through my life. I believe my confidence came from these things.

The people around me believed in me, loved me, and spoke life to me and around me. God created me, and I walk this earth choosing to understand that.

Are there times when my sense of knowing is shaken? Absolutely. Has confidence been misplaced at times, and have I hurt people? Undoubtedly. Have I, like everyone else, had to find my voice amid insecurity and pain? Yes. But through all of that there has been this seed planted deep within my soul that took root inside my heart and captivated my mind. I remind myself daily that I am here for a reason. My confidence rests in the knowledge that I was planned, and there is a purpose in my life that is greater than anything I could possibly imagine. My confidence comes from the knowledge that God resides in me. With every breath, every conversation, and every heartbeat, I have the opportunity to let the glory of God manifest in my daily life, and you do too.

We can manifest the glory of God with our smiles, kind words, simple acts of goodness, and in sharing the beauty around us. His glory is in the sky, the waves, and the sand between your toes. It's in the laughter of children. It's woven through the colors of the rainbow and the gentle sway of the trees in the wind. It's in our stories. It's bubbling on the surface for some, and for others it's buried deep beneath pain and hurt, yet for all of us, we get the opportunity with each new day to let others see who they are meant to be by showing them who they are to us.

You see, my confidence comes from God, but it is built and nurtured through the words, actions, protection, and strength of my family and friends. It comes from the incredible people who have graced the pages and stages of my life and those who have taken the time to see me, hear me, and walk with me.

To my reader—my friend, I see you. I listen to you, and you are magnificent. You are beautiful. You are more than the words that have been spoken to you or over you. You are more than the things that have been done to you. You are created from love for love. If you are feeling weak today, allow me to speak to your soul. Allow my words to sink into the depths of you. I hear you. I see you. I'm with you.

The Joy of the Lord Is My Strength

It would make sense for me to say that I wish I could tell my children no harm will ever come to them and every day will be filled with rainbows, butterflies, unicorns, and fairies. But actually, I don't. I don't wish those things at all because I've seen how challenges play a part in making us who we are, and through it all, we will stand. The important part is that you must remind yourself you will come through it, and the beauty is that in the midst of it all—the good, the bad, and the ugly, you will grow.

We need to learn, then, how to find our peace during it all. We do this by understanding we aren't in control, and we can't adjust the dials to make it all better. What we can do is find our peace right in the middle of it and never let it go.

I once had someone tell me to never lose my joy because the joy of the Lord is my strength. For a while, it was something that I really held on to. Being someone who is predisposed to joy, that kind of thinking served me well. For a while, this lost some of the flair for me, but over the course of the last three years, I have renewed that thinking. I have come to know that God is my peace, and in and through God, my peace is real. As my focus is toward God, and I reach out in that direction, I realize there is something greater at play in my life—not because I'm in control but almost because of just the opposite.

I am relinquishing control, acknowledging God, and in this process my peace is restored. I think this is what it means to not just have joy but the joy of the Lord. If I could be in control and dictate how life would go, my joy would be good enough, but since I can't do that, I must have God's joy and surrender control to Him. The joy of the Lord is my strength, and peace is found in the letting go.

Embrace the Reality and Stand in the Truth

Peter, my brother with Down Syndrome, is a beautiful man who is not without his challenges. Our family has had forty-two years of enjoying Peter's life, but if I'm honest, there are times when we have become "all Petered out."

I realize that sounds harsh, but imagine being with someone who asks you the same question no less than two hundred and twelve times a day, and the question is, "Do you love me?" or "Do you hate me?" or "Who's going to take me to a movie?" Those are true examples of some of the questions he asks every day—over and over again.

Then there is the emotional roller coaster he's on at times. He, like all of us, negotiates good days, bad days, hormonal changes, midlife crises, and all the rest. The difference is he doesn't process these things the same way we do despite his very high emotional intelligence. There is a lag in his processing, so there are added levels of complexity to his life.

As our family gets older, we find ourselves amazed by everything Peter has walked through in his life. The rest of us have worked with therapists or counselors, but unfortunately for Peter, there aren't many counselors who help people with Down Syndrome, so he ends up doing his best to process life the best way he can. We are astounded at his resilience despite his challenges.

Like me, Peter has been celebrated from the time he was conceived. When the questions about his "condition" (which was how they referred to autism in the 1970s) were first acknowledged, he has been embraced. He is who he is, and by embracing the beauty of him, by standing in the truth of who he is, it has been well with our souls.

Peter is extraordinary. He is exactly who he is meant to be—one less chromosome and all. And he rocks that missing chromosome! The same is true with anything. The moment we *embrace reality*

choose to embrace reality and stand in the truth of whatever we are facing, the easier it is for our hearts and minds to align and make it well with our souls. Peter and others like him should be celebrated—not tolerated. We can learn so much from these extraordinary people.

A Practice from The Gathering Cloud

Retreating to Be Well in Your Soul

1. Find a quiet space.

2. Consider how you care for yourself. You feed yourself; you rest your body with sleep; you clothe yourself, and you provide a living space for yourself.

3. Express to God in prayer your desires to be well, happy, peaceful, and loved.

4. Think of someone you love. Express to God in prayer your desires for them to be well, happy, peaceful, and loved.

5. If you are able, recall someone who has hurt you or whom you have hurt. As best as you can, bless that person and express to God in prayer your desires for them to be well, happy, peaceful, and loved.

6. Conclude by saying, "God, thank you for showing your mercy and lovingkindness to all people."

11

SOLITUDE AND THE DESERT

Solitude is the furnace of transformation.
Without solitude we remain victims of our society
and continue to be entangled in the illusions of
the false self…. Solitude is the place of the great
struggle and the great encounter—the struggle
against the compulsions of the false self, and the
encounter with the loving God who offers himself
as the substance of the new self.

—HENRI NOUWEN[27]

Imagine you are in the desert—to be found in quiet stillness and to belong to yourself. I have begun to research the Desert Fathers, who were early Christian hermits, ascetics, and monks who lived mainly in the Scetes desert of Egypt beginning around the third century AD. I want to learn about the Desert Fathers to understand the underpinnings of my faith and to explore the mystery of how stillness and quiet can lead to peace, a life of lovingkindness, and the experience of my true, full self by letting go of myself.

The beauty of stillness gets lost amidst busy schedules and binge-watching. Days in the desert offer the space to breathe deeply from within the core of our being. These days are grounding, rich, dense, yet alone, still, and quiet. Then there are days in the rainforest where you come together and commune, where you meet face-to-face and celebrate. Both kinds of days are filled with spiritual nutrients that heal and waken parts of ourselves that have been quiet for too long. Both experiences push us into a space of engagement where we understand that our boundaries will be pushed, and we may feel uncomfortable, but I assure you both spaces provide the proper nutritional makeup for growth and maturity.

Loneliness takes many forms, and I think we often equate loneliness with being alone. But in fact, the opposite can be just as true. Loneliness can happen in a marriage, or a large family made up of many siblings, or in friendships, parenting, and dating. Some of the loneliest people are the ones you wouldn't expect to ever be lonely at all.

Loneliness has nothing to do with being alone and everything to do with feeling alone. We can be in solitude and never feel lonely. In fact, in the quiet of solitude, we can discover things we may have never found while surrounded by people—regardless of how lovely they may be.

Alone in the Wilderness

Imagine you are alone in the wilderness. My nephew was once completing his cadet training in Canada, and one of the challenges he had to endure was a twenty-four-hour period in the wilderness while alone and unarmed.

I'm not sure how much you know about Canadian wildlife, but it contains some significant creatures that could kill you in an instant: grizzly bears, brown bears, cougars, and wolves, just to name a few. I recall him telling me that as part of their survival gear, they all had a whistle, and if memory serves me correctly, maybe a flashlight.

The instructions were that if you heard the whistle blow, you ran as fast as you could to the assigned gathering point or muster station because the blow of a whistle meant trouble somewhere. He made it through the night, and in my opinion, he is one of the bravest people I know. I'm certain I wouldn't have lasted beyond the appearance of the first star in the night sky.

Being alone in the wilderness can be a scary place, but it can also be a rich experience if we allow ourselves to fully embrace it. Life today is busy for most of us. I know that I fall into the busy category, and to be completely honest, I enjoy being busy. I like a life that is full yet laced with protected space for family and friends.

Time alone seems to have lost its appeal, or maybe the appeal isn't gone so much as the determination to carve out the space to actually be alone. The offer of things to fill our time and keep us occupied is always just a click or swipe away. We have Netflix, On Demand TV, and social media platforms with people up and ready to chat at any hour. Like you, I love all of these comforts, but I am amazed at how we have become reliant on sound and content to stimulate us. I'm always amazed at the countless babies in strollers that I see who are occupied by the latest app rather than the color of the leaves on the trees. Have we become so addicted to entertainment that we are no longer content with ourselves?

We need to remember that being alone can be a healing experience. Sherrie Bourg Carter, PsyD, psychologist, and author of *High Octane Women: How Superachievers Can Avoid Burnout*, specializes in women and stress. In her article in *Psychology Today*, she shares six benefits to spending time alone:

1. Solitude allows you to reboot your brain and unwind.

2. Solitude helps to improve concentration and increase productivity.

3. Solitude gives you an opportunity to discover yourself and find your own voice.

4. Solitude provides time for you to think deeply.

5. Solitude helps you work through problems more effectively.

6. Solitude can enhance the quality of your relationships with others.[28]

If you take a moment to reflect on the above reasons, I think we can all agree that spending time alone and creating a space for ourselves is paramount to our holistic health. Turning off all the external sound bytes and white noise that clutter our minds and hearts is beneficial.

Time spent alone is a time of learning. The story of the night my nephew spent in the wilderness has stayed with me for years. I'm not entirely sure what the objective was, but I'm confident that his time in the wilderness did more for him than what he has shared. I'm sure as the years progress he will think back on that night and draw on the experience. Similarly, myself and my girlfriends have found that by being alone, we have found ourselves.

A Practice from The Gathering Cloud

Retreating to Be in Solitude

1. Set aside a few minutes to meditate on this Scripture: "Be still and know that I am God" (Psalm 46:10 NIV). Repeat this verse to yourself a few times. Rest in the awe of these words and consider the magnitude of that truth that we can be completely still and experience God.

2. Then say these words out loud: "Be still and know that I am." Again, rest in these words. Don't rush, but allow time for the words to saturate your heart and soul.

3. Then reflect on these words: "Be still and know." Consider that we can know God—confidently, boldly, and strongly from a place of stillness and awe.

4. Then go further and find God's peace as you say, "Be still."

5. Lastly, meditate on the fact that God wants you to simply *be*. Know that you are exactly where you're meant to be, resting in the presence of a God of love who simply asks you to be. You are more than your life experiences, more than your hurt, more than what anyone thinks or says of you. You are more than enough in God.

12

TRUE YOU

We have the choice of two identities:
the external mask that seems to be real ...
and the hidden, inner person who seems to us
to be nothing, but who can give herself eternally
to the truth in whom she subsists.

—THOMAS MERTON[29]

Do you know any songs that grip you every time you hear them? One song that does this to me is "The Search" by Joel McKerrow & The Mysterious Few. Whenever I hear it, I fall right into the words as though they are spoken about me. I become the girl in the song who's searching the edges of the world to find herself. I see the valleys, deserts, oceans, and beyond that are all part of the journey. I let go of the shattered dreams, mire, and mud, and leap into the arms of God, a lover who embraces me and leads me to my true self. I chase freedom, run like I've never felt the sun on my face before, follow truth as my map, and in the end, I find myself—my real self, as I was born to be.

This song is about me, and it's about you, and that's why I love it. We are all on this journey. We are pushing through the deserts to find the oceans of abundance. We continue to chase the sunsets knowing every one of them will make the gray days easier to endure.

It is a process to find ourselves. It won't happen without God, and it won't happen without being honest about ourselves, our pasts, and our hurts. Through it all, we pursue truth—not just the truth of what has happened to us or the choices we regret but the truth of who we are in our connectedness to one another and to God.

Go Where You're Celebrated, Not Tolerated

Oftentimes I think we try to change ourselves so that we fit a mold that makes others more comfortable with our lives. I've seen this time and time again, not only in my own life but also in the lives of those around me. It's a soul-sucking experience. It reminds me of Scrat, the squirrel from the movie *Ice Age* who has been chasing that blasted acorn for years and never seems to grab it. Just when it comes within reach, it's gone, and he begins the chase once again.

I've decided that life is much better when you find yourself in places where you are celebrated and not tolerated. Life is too short to be tolerated. That just seems sad. But to do this, we need to be brave enough to look at our current situations and consider whether we need to remove ourselves or risk a time of going it alone until we find our people.

In my life, I was born the third of five children. As I've mentioned, I was born following the death of my older brother, so when the day came for my arrival, everyone was excited. My siblings were anxiously awaiting the birth of their little brother or sister, and my parents held their breath. I was welcomed into the world with balloons, party poppers, and signage declaring,

"She's Arrived!" My entrance into the world was craved, and with my life came a healing of deep sadness. My vulnerable cry as an eight-pound baby girl carried great celebration and healing to a family.

Through all this, I was given an incredible gift: My life was celebrated. Knowing this compels me to place value on people and to celebrate individuals and to let them know they matter. If you find yourself in a place where you aren't being celebrated, dust off your feet and move on. I want to be clear that not *every* day of my life has been party poppers and balloons. In fact, the day of my birth was probably the only day I've literally experienced that, and I wasn't even able to take it in; I was a crying baby who needed tending to every moment.

What I will say is that you know when you are being tolerated—whether it be in a friendship group, a romantic relationship, or within your community or church setting. It's that feeling that crawls up on the inside when you arrive and when you try to engage in conversation, or when you notice social media posts and things you haven't been invited to, and you're unsure as to why. Sometimes these indicators are loud and clear, and other times they are a little less obvious, perhaps even passive-aggressive.

Whatever the case, go where you are celebrated. Find your tribe. Find your people and don't be afraid to do it alone if needed. I've heard Dr. Phil say that if you're in a relationship that is causing you to be less than who you know you are, then the cost is too high. Don't let others make you feel less. Be who you were meant to be and find a place where you are celebrated and not tolerated.

You Are Worth Finding Your Tribe

All that's easy to say, but how does one actually do it? It's scary, and sometimes people stay in bad situations simply because the thought of making a change is so daunting that staying—even when it means not being seen, heard, or valued—seems like a better option.

But if we are going to live in the truth—owning the bad and the good and pursuing God's best in and through us, how can we afford to stay with people who only accept us for who they want us to be? We have to choose which of these dynamics we want. Even in saying that, I can't imagine any of us prefer being fake over being true to ourselves. It's just a question of how badly we want that truth, and how ready we are to leave the fake behind.

Is it risky? Yes.

Will you find your people immediately? Probably not.

Is it worth it? Absolutely.

Whenever you choose to look for your tribe, start by spending some time with yourself and really evaluating what fuels you. What are your likes and dislikes? As you do this, you may discover that you've been spending time in places or with people you're not even interested in.

For example, I love camping, and wherever we live, I make it a priority to find my camping tribe. This tribe includes people who like talking by a fire into the wee hours of the morning and who don't mind the challenges of the outdoors. They value nature, space, and time with family that doesn't involve any other stimulation than nature, dirt, and stars. I didn't realize this about myself until I was well into my thirties. That's a simple example of how I spent time learning about myself and then set out to discover those who loved the same things and found a community and a space to be celebrated. What is it for you? We are complex individuals, and it's imperative we learn about ourselves, so we can place ourselves in life-giving communities and relationships.

My sixteen-year-old son loves video games. He loves to play with friends both near and far, and they spend hours yelling at the screen and at each other through their headsets and gear. I, on the other hand, hate video games and find them an absolute waste of time. Because of my dislike for this activity, my son and I were at odds with one another.

I was constantly yelling at him to get off his games, not understanding (or really caring) that he could be in the middle of a game, and his departure would let down his team. He would, of course, be angry with me for forcing him to quit prematurely. Finally, much to my chagrin, I decided to spend some time talking to him about his games, why he gets so angry with me, and vice versa. He explained to me about mid-game departures and how that affected his team. It made sense to me, so we needed to create a system that worked for both of us. We developed one, and it usually works.

Something else I learned about his games is that he found a community where he is celebrated, and although he didn't know every person, he found a tribe where he could be fully himself— headset and all. Much like my camping crew, he found a specialized group he enjoyed. I needed to understand and place value on that.

Going South after Thirty-Three

Another element of finding a tribe that celebrates you is learning to celebrate yourself. A lot of women worry about aging. They worry about losing their looks and what might happen as their bodies and minds age. But let me tell you, what I discovered through my interviews is that there is a lot to celebrate when it comes to aging.

Sure, life does change in your mid-thirties and even more so in your forties. Our breasts seem slightly less perky, lines form around our eyes, and we develop that crinkly skin on our chest; that has to be the worst! We find ourselves repeating things over and over and sounding more and more like our mothers, whom we now realize were absolute saints and did an extraordinary job. All the things we found irritating about our moms in our younger years now seem more like wisdom.

We've discovered things like Poise pads and acknowledge that after three kids, our bladders certainly aren't as strong as they once were and jumping on a trampoline isn't the wisest decision post-babies. We've found random hairs (or whiskers) that appear in unsightly places literally overnight. Our hormonal changes have turned us into emotional rollercoasters. We've bled through everything at least once and have a new appreciation for women who wear white jeans with confidence. We know they have either had a hysterectomy, or they are insane risk-takers. We've discovered sex really is something amazing, and we are way better at it in our forties—even with the extra kilos and wrinkles.

We've finally realized we are adults who make grown-up decisions every day, and we still giggle at the notion that we are referring to ourselves as grown-ups. We relive the eighties by singing into a brush the moment we hear "Jessie's Girl." "Don't Stop Believin'" is one of our anthems because we know so much more is left in our tanks, and we have so much more to give. Most of us have lived the past ten years sleep deprived and have survived on caffeine and chocolate.

We heated up our babies' bottles in the microwave and now deal with the angst of BPA warnings. Our memories aren't what they once were. In fact, during the interviews for the book, many women shared their fear of losing their minds. The demands of family coupled with work, a social life, and other countless external demands were taking their toll on the memories of most women in this age category.

Taking all this change into consideration and after countless interviews, it was with pleasure that I told each woman they weren't alone. Their concerns were shared by countless others, and I think (or at least hope) that brought them some degree of peace of mind. I know it did for me.

We are changing, and things are going south and every other

direction possible. What we all seem to be learning, though—and this was something extraordinary that came out of the conversations during the research phase of this book—is that we don't care. From our mid-forties on, thankfully, we begin to see each other more as brave souls than like anything we may have seen in the past. We no longer look at the external. We look deeper, and we see clearer. We see our friends almost more like words written across their lives—words like brave, strong, courageous, wise, gracious, and kind.

We see words like this because we have some life behind us. We've watched someone walk through the pain of a divorce and then put themselves back together like a mosaic more beautiful than before. Some have lost children either to unforeseen accidents or the horrible darkness of drugs and substance abuse. We've held each other when we've felt scared. We've felt the pain of cancer and loss, and we've cried together through pain and joy. We've danced, we've sung, and we've loved. It's through this lens that we now look at each other.

Aging with Beauty

The world won't tell you of the beauties of aging. We live in a world of filters. Do you want a whiter smile or sharper features? Are you trying to hide wrinkles, fine lines, dull skin, blemishes, acne, or paleness? There's an app for all of that. We can change anything and easily shave off twenty years of life to give you a younger, fresher look, and it's all done with a few clicks and simple digital tricks.

What's so wrong with aging? Why do we hunger and search for youth, yet when life gets hard, we run for the wise? Why are we compelled to make everything look perfect, whether that be our face, body, or the pictures of our homes we post on Instagram?

I was amazed by the number of women I interviewed who

struggled deeply with what they saw on Instagram or Facebook. If you pull back the filters that gloss every picture, we know that not everything is perfect, but what is perfection anyway? Perfection is a never-ending road. It messes with our hearts, minds, and ultimately our souls. And when it comes to our lives and aging, maybe we shouldn't erase the story our lines tell.

We need to redefine what aging with beauty looks like. There is something beautiful about a man or a woman with lines on their face. I think the natural process of aging is designed to show us that life will be okay; we will get through whatever we're facing if we keep walking. Speaking for myself, watching my mother, grandmothers, aunts, and older friends helps me understand "this too shall pass." The stories of their lives are written on their faces—in their smiles or in their frowns.

Sophia, true to her name, spoke profound wisdom to me when she was the tender age of eleven. We were sitting on her bed and talking about life, and she started to tell me how much she liked her English teacher. Sophia always talked about her teacher's smile and how she had such happy lines on her face. She also spoke of her grandmothers and the joy on their faces. She said that even as their faces rested, they always looked happy.

Sophia asked about plastic surgery and the pursuit of youthfulness. She talked about the lines on both her teacher's face and her grandmother's faces and how, through the lines, she knew life would be okay. She could tell they had stories to tell, whether their stories be of triumph or painful loss. She could see life written on their faces, and the lines gave her courage.

She wondered what a world without laugh lines and wrinkles would look like—faces without lines of truth, victory, kindness, and grace. She wondered if there would be a path to follow or a road that would lead her through the valleys of life. She loved their faces, and with every smile or furrowed brow she saw security and confidence. The lines told her that she could handle whatever life threw her way, and that she too would have the strength she saw in these women. It was obvious to her that these lovely women had chosen not to erase the stories on their faces.

Hands also tell a story. I remember visiting Korea with my husband to see his aunt. Her hands and my mother-in-law's hands were interesting to me. They were sisters, and you could see the stories of their lives written across the beauty of their hands, which were truly the tales of two very different life experiences. Both women's hands were equally beautiful; I could see hardship, pain, and challenge, yet also joy, happiness, and honesty.

We need to let our stories be seen and told. If we erase the beauty of aging, we rob a generation from standing on the challenges we've overcome. Let's not erase the stories of our lives or use filters on the truth of who we are.

Live Your One Life Well

We get one opportunity to live, and life is for living. So often we find ourselves wishing or hoping for a life other than the one we have. Or we find ourselves revisiting our history and living in the past. I've heard this described best by my mentor, Alicia Britt Chole, who refers to this behavior as "peripheral reality," which is living yet longing for another time or space. Longing for what we once had or don't have robs us of what is already right in front of us. It's so easy to do, and it's a trap we've all been caught in at one time or another. I know I certainly have.

I find this conversation shifting in society though. With the rise in popularity of tiny houses and minimalist lifestyles, I hear less of a wishing-we-had-more dialogue. In fact, people are letting go of their need for stuff and their desire to live in excess. People no longer seem to crave these things.

I once had the opportunity to work with Oprah's decluttering expert, Peter Walsh. We've worked together a few times, and it's always been a pleasure. Peter is an exceptional man who places value on everyone he meets. It was an honor to share a platform with him and to have him invest in our projects.

Peter shared that whenever he went head to head with someone who was holding onto things and living in the past, he would go into their house, find a pile of newspapers or magazines, and pull something from the bottom of the pile. He would find the date on the magazine or newspaper, look the person in the eye, and ask them what happened around that time in their lives. In most cases, their stories would unfold and their tears would begin to flow. Peter knew something had caused the person he was working with to have stopped living.

As a mentor, Alicia regularly helps people work their way out of peripheral living. Both Peter and Alicia help people begin to live again. Peter deals with physical clutter, which he says always leads to mental and emotional clutter. Alicia deals with soul clutter, which can have the opposite effect and then result in physical clutter. Both experts are dealing with matters of the heart and individuals who, due to traumatic experiences, have stopped living.

We have one life. It's important we allow ourselves to live it.

Disappointment Accepts Reality

Sometimes life is disappointing. Sometimes people are disappointing (there, I said it). It's true, and it's something we need to recognize and live through. Disappointment can happen every day if we let it. Here's the thing about disappointment that can help take the sting out of it and help you process it: Disappointment is simply your expectations being unmet. This means you have a plan, and either people don't or life doesn't deliver on that expectation, so you're left disappointed.

According to Dr. Mary Lamia, disappointment is one of the most profound ways to experience sadness.[30] Disappointment can spiral into sadness, and then sadness into self-doubt. Surprisingly fast, we can begin to wonder, *Who am I?* We can lose our sense of self.

How do we tackle disappointment? In one of my sessions with Alicia, she asked me to identify a time when I felt disappointed. I decided to focus on a time between Philip and me. I shared the disappointment with Alicia, and she took me down a path asking the question of why. Why was I disappointed in that situation? Then she had me ask why again, then again, then again. She made me keep drilling down until it was painfully obvious to me that, in fact, it wasn't the situation at all that caused the disappointment. What caused it was my expectation of the situation.

The *why* behind the *what* always matters. Going down the path of why wasn't at all comfortable. It was actually revealing and left me quite vulnerable, but it helped me understand that it was more about me than it was about Philip.

Another thing Alicia helped me see was that letting people know that we are disappointed with them really does nothing for anyone. It doesn't help the person you're disappointed with because knowing you're disappointed with them only makes them feel bad. And other than maybe getting something off your chest, it doesn't move you toward reconciling your relationship, mending the conflict, or healing your hurt.

So, what does all this mean? It means our greatest defense against disappointment is to own our expectations and accept reality. Reality is just that: It's real and acknowledging what is happening or not happening allows you the opportunity to stand in it and ask the *why* questions, which drills down to the core of the disappointment. In saying that, the disappointment doesn't necessarily always land back on you either. In some of my cases, my disappointment landed toward God. I was mad at God. And guess what? God's big enough to carry and deal with my anger and disappointment from unmet expectations.

We find our being, and we live in the soft arms of who we

really are. Find yourself a pen and a piece of paper, write down what you are disappointed with, and keep asking the question of why. When you arrive at an answer, ask why again. Drill down until you come to the bottom of the matter because that is where we will find ourselves and find freedom. It was at the bottom of my disappointment that I realized although Philip was the circumstance, it was God I had an issue with, and then I was able to let go and find freedom.

If you find your disappointment is with God, invariably it means you aren't seeing the situation in full clarity. God is always love, and love will always be working for your best. You can ask God to show you how love was working, even through the disappointment of what happened. The pain you feel is still true, and it still matters, but discovering where God was at work in your circumstance will help you forgive and find healing.

Who Do You Think You Are?

When our kids were young, I asked them, "What do you want to be when you grow up?" As they got older and had more of an understanding about life, my question shifted from that fun, imaginative world to a more introspective one: "Who do you want to be?" I've used this to help them make decisions. It's also a great question for when they have done something wrong and discipline was required.

Who do you want to be, and what do you want to be known for? These are great questions that let them consider themselves and the world around them from more of a macro view. Additionally, this is a good question for us to ask of ourselves.

I found it interesting that most people seem to struggle with a deep sense of unknowing when it comes to who they are. As we get older, the question remains, but the answer seems to get tangled and twisted into more of an answer of, "What do you do?" It's almost like we have to recite our résumé in order to qualify for a conversation. What you do, although interesting and valuable, pales in comparison to who you are—in my opinion. What makes you tick? What is inside you and yet to be discovered? Who do you think you are?

When I was in first grade, I had an interesting teacher. Some would call him eccentric, or maybe creative, but I found him odd. As a young girl, I remember thinking that the way he chose to discipline us as students was bizarre. One day, we were in the classroom, and he was annoyed about something we'd done. We were all huddled around a cymbal that used to hang from the roof, and he would use a drum stick to hit it (much like a gong) to get our attention. On this particular day, he was in a foul mood, and I must have done something to upset him because after hitting the drumstick on the gong, he gave me a huge whack across the head with the drumstick. You can imagine how much that hurt both my head and my pride. Wow, what a blow!

I stood up to him that day. I remember pulling together all my six years of strength and courage and told him what he did was wrong. I think I took him (and probably my class) by surprise. In his flamboyant way, he stormed out of the classroom and headed for the principal's office. I knew I was in trouble, and I had to accept what would be coming my way. I certainly wasn't prepared for what happened after that, which would shape some of the foundational stones of my life.

From the principal's office, the teacher called my mom to inform her what had happened, and he told her he was going to knock some of the confidence out of me. I anticipated getting in trouble from my mom, as she typically sided with the teacher. She usually erred on the side of assuming wrongdoing on our parts unless proven innocent. This time, however, I don't know if it was my teacher's tone, the words he used, or what, but his offer to knock the confidence out of me ignited a fire within my mom's belly. The mama bear had been poked, and she was ready to roar!

My mom showed up at school that day and made her presence known. She firmly dealt with the matter face-to-face. From that point on, it was abundantly clear to me I could challenge authority in a respectful way. My voice mattered, and I mattered. That day, after being hit over the head with a drumstick and publicly humiliated, my brave mother gave me my confident voice because she saw me, knew me, and loved me.

Who do I think I am? I am Susan. I am strong yet soft and tender. I am confident and feeling. I am courageous and brave. I am kind, and I am a child of God created by love and for love. I'm funny, and I love to laugh. I am planned, and I was handpicked for such a time as this. I am living the best life I can, and I still make mistakes. I am me, and I am alive because I am found in God, and God is found in me. That's who I am, and it's from that place that I love, live, and breathe.

I wonder how you describe yourself. Who do you think you are? Is your inner narrative one of self-loathing, hate, and lack? Do you criticize yourself faster than you can smile at yourself? Do you look in the mirror and love who is looking back at you, or do you avoid mirrors altogether? Do you shrink back because you've been told you're not enough, or that you don't measure up? Do you hide behind labels and job descriptions, praying that you're never asked a question beyond, "What do you do?" Who are you?

Our internal narrative is so important, and we need to check it regularly. We need to acknowledge that we are body, soul, and spirit, and we can't ignore any of the three. We need to speak to our soul, our spirit, and our body in an honoring way. We need to stop the damning talk that is happening in our head and replace it with healthy words—words of life that celebrate who we are.

Beyond Ego

I have spent the better part of the last twenty years writing and speaking about identity—who you are, in context of whose you are: God's. I was raised with a healthy sense of self-esteem from which I confidently strode through life. But innately, I had a consistent sense of fear. Perhaps it was the fact that my father had so many heart attacks throughout my childhood. Perhaps it was the loss of my infant brother whom I never knew.

In any case, in the last two years, everything I have known about identity has been unexpectedly deconstructed and transformed. Everything I have known about my identity are social and psychological constructs: a "small" self or "false" self. My true, greater self—which is rooted in the truth that God lives in me—is the source from which I should be living my life.

We often describe ourselves like a biography or a résumé. We are full of labels and details: our name, age, family of origin, spouse, children, values, beliefs, hopes, dreams, location, what we've done, who we know, who we are friends with, who are our enemies, our likes, our dislikes, what we look like, what we sound like, what tribe or group we identify with, and the list goes on—like the ingredients and nutrition labels on a processed food product. We derive much value in cultivating and defending this ego and consider it our identity.

But we are more. You are more. I am more. For in the quiet stillness of the very core of my being, and with each passing day, I am becoming more aware of and more present to God's presence within me and God's presence around me. To be truly human and to be truly ourselves, we are to become what God is: love.

We are made from love and for love, and we are made in the image and likeness of God who is love. This love does not ask for anything. It does not seek the things that drive us in life: safety and security, power and control over people and things, love and esteem. Love is what renowned contemplative teacher Fr. Thomas Keating often calls our "emotional programs for happiness."[31] The false self, often wounded in childhood, processes in the subconscious the physical, emotional, and spiritual traumas of our life.

Throughout this inner journey of contemplative practices, the judgments and separations of life decline, and inclusion, acceptance, and (most importantly) surrender replace them. We begin living out of our hearts and not our minds as holistic beings instead of minds carried around by bodies.

In this space and in this journey, I have found acceptance from a loving God and acceptance of myself—warts and all, I've found acceptance of others. Hopefully, I continue to grow in compassion and lovingkindness. It's as if I not only showed up and became present, but I've also woken up to something mysterious yet undeniable, and now I'm finally starting to grow up.

As Richard Rohr elegantly states in *Falling Upward*, "There is nothing to prove and nothing to protect. I am who I am, and it's enough."[32] This connectedness and oneness has become a real source of life to me, that God is in me, but also that I am in God. This is the journey of connectedness waiting for each one of us.

Books like Henri Nouwen's *The Way of the Heart*, and my mentor, Alicia Britt Chole's, *Anonymous*, and almost any of Richard Rohr's books examine true self-identity. I encourage you to read their words, and I'm confident this spiritual path will transform your spiritual practice as it has mine.

It's fitting to close this book with a quote from the American mystic Fr. Thomas Merton, who says it so well in his book, *Love and Living*: "Love is our true destiny. We do not find the meaning of life by ourselves alone—we find it with one another."[33] May you find this destiny as you seek God to find your true you!

A Practice from The Gathering Cloud

Retreating to Discover True Self

1. Set aside ten minutes in your day. Find a quiet space and a mirror, preferably one you do not have to hold. Stand or sit in front of a mirror close enough so that you can clearly see your face, as if you were going to apply makeup or brush your teeth.

2. Pray, "God, come be with me in this place."

3. Look in the mirror and notice the physical features of your face—your eyes, nose, mouth, ears, the shape and wrinkles. Try not to judge if you look good or not; just observe your face.

4. As you look at your reflection, imagine that your reflection is God looking at you, gazing from His Spirit and seeing your spirit, knowing you and being with you.

5. Express your gratitude for how lovingly God has created you, inside and out. Smile at yourself and experience God's smile upon you and your life.

ACKNOWLEDGMENTS

Philip, I knew from the moment I met you that an adventure was about to begin. Thank you for seeing me, for celebrating me, and for choosing us. Thank you for being one of the brave ones who isn't afraid to face the dark side of life and come through refined and beautiful.

To my children, you have my heart forever, and if there is one thing I know for certain it's that your dad and I got three really great things right in life, and it's you three. Sophia, you made me a mum. Thank you for being part of the writing team and for sharing your gift and love for words with me. Gabriel, your entertainment, enlightening conversation, and Uber driving has helped me complete this. Ella, your encouragement and interest in my work propels me forward.

To my writing crew, wow. We did it! Thank you, Philip, Sophia, Jane, Ashley, Caitlin, Deborah, Jo, Anna, Phoebe, and Lizzie, for encouraging me, reading, commenting, and the laughs. You kept me sane. To David, Bill, Nina, Jeanna, and the entire BroadStreet team, thanks for saying yes to me. David, thank you for being patient and holding my hand through this. You are a gentleman and a wordsmith. Nathanael, thank you for your work and capturing my voice so beautifully. To Nicole, thank you for believing and telling me I could when I thought I couldn't. This book wouldn't be without your willingness to open doors and invite me in; you inspired me and encouraged me to do this project. I'm forever grateful.

To my family, my mother who has taught me how to live, laugh, and love, there are no words to tell you how grateful I am to be your daughter. I adore you. To my late father, I miss your wisdom and influence in my life every day. To my siblings who have had my back from our first hello, you are my safe place, and I've loved learning how to live with you. Thanks for always having your boots on.

To the countless others who added to this, encouraged me, and asked me how it was going, thank you for listening and caring.

To the women who shared their truth with me, you wrote this with me. I thought about you throughout the entire process. You are the brave ones, and I hold your truth with honor.

To the God whom I abide in and who abides in me.

With love, respect, and gratitude,
Susan

Notes

1   Brené Brown, *Rising Strong* (New York: Penguin Random House, 2015), 267.

2   C. H. Spurgeon, *Spurgeon's Gems* (London: Alabaster & Passmore, 1855), 155.

3   Johannes (Sarracenus) *Metalogicon of John of Salisbury: A Twelfth-Century Defense of the Verbal and Logical Arts of the Trivium* (Berkeley and Los Angeles: University of California Press, 1955), 167.

4   Paul Tillich, Sermon, 2012.

5   Eric Klinenberg, "Is Loneliness a Health Epidemic?," *New York Times*, February 9, 2018, https://www.nytimes.com/2018/02/09/opinion/sunday/loneliness-health.html.

6   Tania De Jong, "Loneliness Is the Global Epidemic of Our Times, *Huffington Post*, May 10, 2016, https://www.huffingtonpost.com.au/tania-de-jong/loneliness-is-the-global-epidemic-of-our-times_a_21544979.

7   Ann Voskamp, *1000 Gifts* (Grand Rapids: Zondervan, 2012), 58.

8   Rollin McCraty, "The Energetic Heart: Bioelectromagnetic Interactions within and between People," *The Neuropsychotherapist* 6 (July 2003), 22.

9   Richard Rohr, *Breathing Under Water* (Cincinnati: St Anthony Messenger Press, 2011), n.p.

10 John Brandon, "The Surprising Reason Millennials Check Their Phones 150 Times a Day," April 17, 2017, https://www.inc.com/john-brandon/science-says-this-is-the-reason-millennials-check-their-phones-150-times-per-day.html.

11 Alyssa Bischmann and Christina Richardson, "Age of First Exposure to Pornography Shapes Men's Attitudes toward Women," 2017, http://www.apa.org/news/press/releases/2017/08/pornography-exposure.aspx.

Notes

12 Martin Daubney, "Men's Lives Are Being Ruined by Pornography. So Why Aren't We Angry about It?," *The Telegraph*, March 29, 2017, https://www.telegraph.co.uk/men/thinking-man/mens-lives-ruined-pornography-arent-angry.

13 Nick Olejniczak, "Brain Activity in Sex Addiction Mirrors That of Drug Addiction," University of Cambridge, July 11, 2014, http://www.cam.ac.uk/research/news/brain-activity-in-sex-addiction-mirrors-that-of-drug-addiction.

14 Simone Kühn and Jürgen Gallinat, "Brain Structure and Functional Connectivity Associated with Pornography Consumption: The Brain on Porn," *JAMA Psychiatry* (2014), 827–34.

15 Elizabeth M. Morgan, "Associations between Young Adults' Use of Sexually Explicit Materials and Their Sexual Preferences, Behaviors, and Satisfaction," *Journal of Sex Research* 48, no. 6 (2011), 520–30.

16 A. J. Bridges, "Pornography's Effect on Interpersonal Relationships," in J. Stoner and D. Hughes, eds., *The Social Costs of Pornography: A Collection of Papers* (Princeton: Witherspoon Institute, 2010), 89–110.

17 A. J. Bridges et al, "Aggression and Sexual Behavior in Best-Selling Pornography Videos: A Content Analysis Update," *Violence against Women* 16, no. 10 (2010), 1065–85.

18 Mental Health America, "Co-Dependency," http://www.mentalhealthamerica.net/co-dependency.

19 Rohr, *Breathing Under Water*, n.p.

20 Fred R. Shapiro, "Who Wrote the Serenity Prayer?" *The Chronicle Review*, April 28, 2014, https://www.chronicle.com/article/Who-Wrote-the-Serenity-Prayer-/146159.

21 Winfried Abel, *The Prayer Book of St. Nicholas of Flue: Mystery of the Center*, Christiana Edition (Stein Am Rhein: 1999).

Notes

22 Zach Williams, "Chainbreaker," Sony/ATV Music Publishing, 2016.

23 Diana Butler Bass, *Grateful: The Transformative Power of Giving Thanks* (San Francisco: HarperOne, 2018), n.p.

24 *People*, "Brooke Shields' Interview with *Life Magazine*," March 22, 2007, http://celebritybabies.people.com /2007/03/22/brooke_shields__4-3.

25 Shakespeare, *Hamlet*, 4.5.43–44.

26 Horatio G. Spafford, "It Is Well with My Soul," 1873.

27 Henri Nouwen, *The Way of the Heart: The Spirituality of the Desert Fathers and Mothers* (New York: HarperOne, 1981).

28 Sherrie Bourg Carter, "Six Reasons You Should Spend More Time Alone," *Psychology Today*, January 31, 2012, https:// www.psychologytoday.com/us/blog/high-octane-women /201201/6-reasons-you-should-spend-more-time-alone.

29 Thomas Merton, *New Seeds of Contemplation* (New York: New Directions Books, 1972), 295.

30 Mary C. Lamia, "Expectation, Disappointment, and Sadness," *Psychology Today*, November 20, 2011, https://www.psychologytoday.com/au/blog/intense-emotions-and-strong-feelings/201111/expectation-sadness-and-disappointment.

31 Thomas Keating, "Thomas Keating's False Self," *Centering Prayer, Psychology & Spirituality*, August 10, 2016, https://www.thecontemplativelife.org/blog/2016/8/10/thomas-keatings-false-self.

32 Richard Rohr, *Falling Upward: A Spirituality for the Two Halves of Life* (San Francisco: Jossey-Bass, 2011), n.p.

33 Thomas Merton, *Love and Living* (New York: Ferrar, Straus, Giroux, 1967), n.p.

ABOUT THE AUTHOR

Susan J. Sohn is a community builder, speaker, w
facilitator, and online/social media entrepreneur. She
scribed as raw, honest, disarming, and immediately rel
san has the ability to gather people and create rich co
Her table is a place where everyone is welcome, every
a voice, and everyone is heard. Raised in the Canadia
ries, her eclectic life has brought her to various cities arou
world. She has worked with influential media companies
as the *New York Times*, as well as significant global not-for-p
and faith-based organizations. Her digital imprint engages
over 650,000 listeners through her podcasts and hundred
millions of social media impressions. From creating busines
to throwing parties, Susan lives a life of joy that makes space f
heartache and insecurity. Susan sees beauty and possibility in th
lives of everyone she meets. She currently resides near Sydney
Australia, with her husband, Philip, and their children, Sophia,
Gabriel, and Ella. Learn more about Susan at getreallive.com.

⌐e GetRealLive Retreat Experience!

⌐ffer time to gather, to connect, and to leave ⌐life you dream of living. Retreats are designed ⌐d. Every moment is intentionally crafted for you ⌐gh and into something new. From the moment you ⌐goal and desire is to treat you, to challenge you, and ⌐ur senses and help you take the next brave step. Check ⌐website to see some of the incredible photos, videos, ⌐ries of those who have taken part in one of our retreats: ⌐/getreallive.com.

"The GetRealLive Retreat was life-changing in every way. ⌐can pinpoint change in my life back to that weekend togeth-er. Everything from the sessions and the food to the surprises throughout our time together was meticulously planned. Susan and her team invest everything into this experience, and it's felt from the time you register until well after you are home. Much more than just a weekend away and an investment worth making."

—Jess